Kumihimo
BASICS&BEYOND

Kumihimo

BASICS&BEYOND

24 braided and beaded jewelry
projects on the kumihimo disk

Rebecca Ann Combs

KALMBACH BOOKS

Kalmbach Books
21027 Crossroads Circle
Waukesha, Wisconsin 53186
www.Kalmbach.com/Books

Published in 2014

18 17 16 15 14   1 2 3 4 5

Manufactured in the United States of America

ISBN: 978-1-62700-043-7
EISBN: 978-1-62700-064-2

Editor: Mary Wohlgemuth
Art Director: Lisa Bergman
Technical Editor: Jane Danley Cruz
Layout Designer: Lisa Schroeder
Photographer: William Zuback

Publisher's Cataloging-in-Publication Data
Combs, Rebecca Ann.
   Kumihimo : basics & beyond : 24 braided and beaded jewelry projects on the kumihimo disk / Rebecca Ann Combs.

      p. : col. ill. ; cm.

   Issued also as an ebook.
   ISBN: 978-1-62700-043-7

   1. Braid–Handbooks, manuals, etc. 2. Beadwork–Patterns. 3. Beadwork–Handbooks, manuals, etc.
   4. Jewelry making–Handbooks, manuals, etc. I. Title.

TT880 .C66 2014
745.594/2

Contents

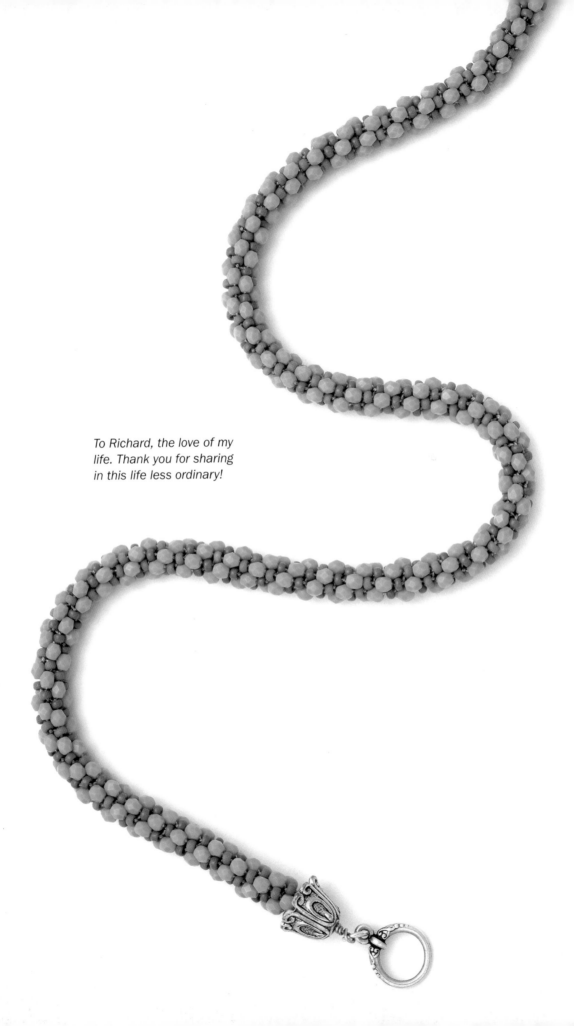

To Richard, the love of my life. Thank you for sharing in this life less ordinary!

Introduction

For me, it all started with a little boy and a braid. I was chatting with my mom on the phone when she asked if I had heard of kumihimo. "Kumi-what?" I responded. She explained that a little boy had come into her variety store and bought some yarn to make friendship bracelets using a foam disk.

I soon found myself tearing into a package containing a round foam disk, neon-colored yarn, and an instruction pamphlet written entirely in Japanese (thankfully there were several diagrams). Following along, I made my first brightly colored kumihimo braid.

To be perfectly honest, I wasn't terribly impressed with the hot pink and lime green acrylic yarn (summer camp throwback, for sure), but it was fun. So I tried again. This time I used hand-dyed silk strings in muted earth tones finished off in sterling caps. And so my obsession began.

It was exciting searching for new fibers to braid: leather, ribbon, embellishment yarn, satin cord. And then beads. I had to try it with beads!

This was in 2009. I started teaching kumihimo classes in my Tucson, Arizona, bead store. One of my earliest class projects, the Classic Elegance necklace, caught on like wildfire. Kumihimo classes started selling out, and I was challenged to develop fresh designs and classes.

It was thrilling to watch the delight on my students' faces as they watched their first braids grow beneath their disks. My love of kumihimo grew as they returned to proudly show off their creations.

Amazed at how many different designs can be made with such simple means, I eagerly sought out all the kumihimo information I could find and studied with the best kumihimo artists around. It's fascinating to me how each artist and teacher brings her own perspective to this medium.

I'm thankful to have encountered so many wonderful students and mentors along the way. Please join me as I share my knowledge and we continue this kumihimo journey together.

— *Rebecca Combs*

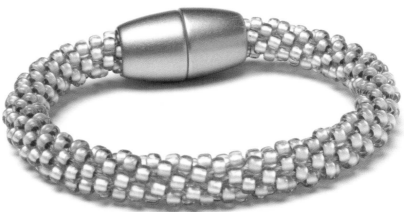

Getting Started

Welcome to your new addiction

You're going to love kumihimo, but I must warn you: Your other hobbies will suffer. So will your housework. Your homework. Whatever other obligations in life you may have.

What is kumihimo?

Kumihimo is traditional Japanese braiding. The techniques go back to the time of the samurai. Next time you're at a museum with a good Asian art collection, look closely at samurai armor and notice the little braids that lace the different sections together. That's kumihimo.

The word kumihimo comes from Japanese terms for gathering or combining cords. It is the name of the technique and also refers to the resulting braid.

While the samurai are long gone, kumihimo lives on. These days in Japan, you'll find kumihimo used for decorative and ceremonial pulls and tassels, embellishments for clothing, and *obi jime* (the belt that ties a kimono shut). With the techniques presented here you could make any of those things, but we'll focus on making jewelry.

HOW TO USE THIS BOOK

The projects in the book are arranged in a skills-building sequence. Be sure to read through and tackle the first project, the Basic Braid, which begins on page 18, to learn the braiding movements that are used for all of the projects in the book.

Subsequent projects add new skills, techniques, and design concepts by building on what you've learned. I highly recommend that you start at the beginning and work your way through. Even if you skip making a project, please read through it so you don't miss any new information.

Measurements are given in inches and yards for fiber and in millimeters for most beads. Online calculators can give you instant conversions, or you can do a little easy math to figure them out. To convert inches to centimeters, multiply the length in inches by 2.54. To convert yards to meters, multiply by .9144.

Basics

BASIC KUMIHIMO TOOLKIT

You don't really need much in the way of tools to get started. The following tools make up the Basic Kumihimo Toolkit. Keep them handy because you'll need them for all the projects. We'll add a few more tools to the kit when we start braiding with beads, but we'll talk about that later.

Japanese braiding stand

Traditional kumihimo is made using a wooden braiding stand called a *marudai*. A marudai is made of a round, smooth piece of wood with a hole in the middle (called a mirror), four wooden legs, and a square wooden base. The fiber you're braiding with is wrapped around weighted wood bobbins called *tama*. To counter the weight of the tama, you hang weights from the braid.

Kumihimo disk

Although I own a marudai and enjoy using it, I learned, and I teach all beginning students, how

The traditional braiding stand is a big investment. You'll be happy to know you can learn kumihimo without buying a marudai!

to braid using a foam kumihimo disk with plastic bobbins. Because the foam does a good job holding medium-weight and heavyweight cords in place, you won't have to worry about weights until you start braiding with beads or doing other projects that use thin cords.

The foam kumihimo disk was invented by Makiko Tada, a Japanese kumihimo master. This inexpensive, easy-to-find disk makes the art of kumihimo much more accessible. You'll find several different brands of kumihimo disks on the market today. Although the differences are slight, some are definitely more durable than others. Look for nice, firm foam. My Hamanaka and BeadSmith brand disks have held up well for several years. Both are white ½"-thick foam disks about 6" in diameter with a 1" hole in the center. The octagonal Kumi-Loom is the same idea in a slightly different shape. There are also mini disks available, which are 3–4" diameter. As long as the disk you use is sturdy ½"-thick foam, you shouldn't have any problems. The BeadSmith mini kumihimo disk fits nicely in my handbag, yet it is sturdy enough to use with beads. The diameter of the disk doesn't affect the size of your braid.

Kumihimo disks usually have a number near each slot, from 1 to 32, so you can follow written patterns in instructional books. We're going to ignore these numbers for now. In fact, the disks in my step-by-step photos don't show numbers at all: I flipped the disk over so that the numbers wouldn't distract us.

Scissors

Any old craft scissors may cut through a single piece of cording, but after you've made an eight-strand braid, you'll be in need of some serious cutting power. Your first braid is going to be 6mm (about ¼") thick. Now is the time to use your sharpest sewing scissors. They need to be able to slice through the braid in a single cut—no hacking!

Binding thread

Before we can cut a braid into pieces, we need to bind the cut end so it doesn't unravel. You can use whatever type of beading thread you have handy. It doesn't matter what color it is because it will be covered with the endcap, and it doesn't need to be particularly strong—just strong enough that it doesn't snap when you try to knot with it. I like Nymo, One-G, or Silamide.

Bobbins

Bobbins are essential on all but the shortest of braids because they keep your braiding fibers tidy and tangle free. The bobbins I like are made of a soft plastic and can be flipped open or closed by pushing on the domed side. When braiding, each fiber or group of fibers that share a bobbin is called a *warp*.

Glue

Some jewelers don't trust glue. They just won't believe that it will hold. I use E6000 glue for all of my braids, and believe me, this magic elixir is strong. Once you've glued an endcap on with E6000, it pretty much takes the strength of Hercules to pry it off again. In addition to being super strong, it's waterproof, dries clear, and doesn't bond to skin.

E6000 has two downsides: it's stinky and it gets thick and goopy relatively quickly after opening it. The first problem is solved by working in a well-ventilated area. The second can be solved by buying only small tubes that you can use up quickly (within a month or two). For a few projects, you'll want to have some white glue (Elmer's glue, for example) on hand.

Calipers

You don't need to keep calipers in your toolkit for projects in this book, because the supply list will call out what size endcap is needed; however, once you start to venture out on your own, this inexpensive tool is your best friend when it comes to choosing the right size endcap for your braid. Look for one that measures in millimeters because that's how most endcaps are labeled. If you can find one with both metric and English measurements, even better. My preferred calipers are digital for easy reading, switch between metric and English with the push of a button, and measure both inside and outside diameter.

Jewelry pliers

These aren't needed at all for the braiding portion of the projects, but you'll want two pairs when it's time to add a clasp. I like to use one pair of bentnose pliers and one pair of chainnose pliers for opening and closing jump rings, but whatever combination of pliers you're used to using will work fine. Also, if your pliers are leaving marks on the jump rings, try coating the jaws with Tool Magic, a liquid rubber.

Scrap paper

Keep a supply of scrap paper near your work area (recycled printer paper is great for this). When it's time to glue, your work surface will thank you.

Toothpick

It may sound trivial, but using a toothpick is the secret to precision glue application.

Wire cutters

You'll need these for snipping excess wire after making a wrapped loop on a cone. If wire-wrapping is not your thing, you can always swap out a cone for a standard endcap with a built-in loop.

Measuring tape

You probably have one of these in your jewelry making stash, so just be sure it's handy.

KUMIHIMO MATH

Before you begin any kumihimo project, first decide on your desired finished length. What are you making? A bracelet? A necklace? A dog leash? You must have a number in mind, because you can't add more thread or cord to your project once started. This isn't like knitting or crochet where you can tie on or splice in additional thread. You must cut at the beginning as much fiber as you'll need for your entire project.

Fear not! There's an easy-to-remember ratio: **You need three times your finished length per warp.**

For example, let's say you want to make an 18" necklace: 18 x 3 = 54. That means you need 54" for each of the eight warps of the braid. (Remember that each fiber or group of fibers that share a bobbin is a warp.) 54" = 1.5 yd., and 1.5 yd. x 8 = 12. That means you need 12 yd. total for the 18" necklace.

Because you can't add more to the project once started, we're using a ratio that's actually pretty generous. Nothing is sadder than running out of cord when you're just a bit short of your target length. The actual amount of material needed will depend on its thickness. Thinner cords have less "uptake" than thicker cords. Individual braiders will also braid with varying tensions and will require differing material allowances; however, if you follow the 3-to-1 rule, you shouldn't come up short. If you're concerned about being frugal with your materials, take good notes about your braiding.

Before starting a project, jot down what type of fiber you're using and how much you cut for each warp. When you're finished, record the final braid length. With that information, you can calculate your own use ratio for each type of material that you like to braid with.

The table below assumes an eight-warp round braid. The starting length of each warp is 54" (1½ yd.). (Please note that these figures are based on my experience, and diameters were measured using a digital caliper. A braider's personal tension can affect the outcome.)

Kumihimo Math Cheat Sheet

Fiber	Finished Length (+/- 2")	Braid Diameter (+/- .5mm)	Endcap Size
Vergata Ribbon	34"	3mm	3–4mm
1mm Satin Rattail	28"	4.5mm	5–6mm
2mm Satin Rattail	24"	5.5mm	6mm
3mm Satin Rattail	24"	7mm	8mm

Basics
BRAIDING FIBERS AND OTHER SUPPLIES

You'll be pleased to know that you can create kumihimo braids with pretty much any fiber you can get your hands on: cording of all sorts, ribbon, yarn, embroidery floss, leather, silk, wire, and more.

Satin cord

The most common U.S.-made satin cord goes by the brand name Rattail and is rayon over a cotton core. This is my recommended fiber for a first braid—it's very easy to work with. It's silky smooth with a lustrous finish, comes in lots of colors, and is widely available. Rattail is available in three sizes: #0, #1, and #2. These roughly correspond to 1mm, 2mm, and 3mm in diameter, and that is how I refer to them throughout the book. I've also heard the various sizes described as bug-tail, mouse-tail, and rattail. Rattail is commonly available in over 40 different colors, but sometimes you'll be lucky enough to come across some hand-dyed varieties in a rainbow of beautiful variegated colors.

You'll also find Chinese-made nylon satin cord. It's a little cheaper, but the texture is less silky, so I don't recommend it. It also tends to braid up thicker than the corresponding size in rayon.

Twisted nylon braiding thread

This is the fiber I use most often when doing beaded kumihimo. C-Lon and Superlon (S-Lon) are the two most common brands, and they're available in a few different thicknesses. Use the size 18 beading cord, which is about .5mm thick, with 8º or 6º seed beads. Go for the micro (.12mm) if using 11º or 15º seed beads. You can also braid with nylon string without beads.

Leather

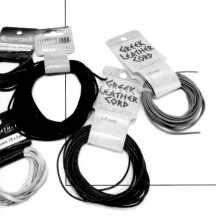

Leather or suede cord can give your braids a masculine look or enhance earthy designs. Quality matters; weak spots can snap, so inspect the leather to make sure it has uniform thickness. For round leather cord, I like 1.5mm Greek leather, but any quality leather at least 1mm in diameter should work well. Leather doesn't condense as much as other fibers, so the resulting braid may be thicker than you anticipate. A basic eight-warp braid made with 1.5mm round leather cord takes a 7mm endcap. For flat leather, I always choose deerskin because it is incredibly soft and smooth. My favorite is called deerskin lace, and it is 3mm wide and just under 1mm thick.

Embroidery floss and pearl cotton

These materials are inexpensive, easy to find, and available in many colors. Embroidery floss and pearl cotton are good choices when you want a braid that's casual, like a friendship bracelet. I also use size 8 pearl cotton when braiding with 11° seed beads.

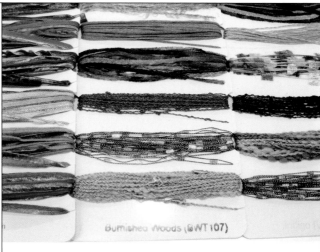

Burnished Woods (BWT107)

Ribbon

This is a category to experiment and have fun with! Ribbon is available in wide range of diameters, fabrics, and finishes. One important thing to keep in mind about ribbon kumihimo is that the finished braid often looks very different from the starting material.

Endcaps and cones

Endcaps are the easiest and most common way to finish kumihimo jewelry. An endcap is basically a hollow tube, generally made of metal, that is capped off at one end and ideally has a loop attached. Cones are another great way to finish off a braid, but because the point of the cone is open, you have to do a little wire wrapping before you use them. Both cones and endcaps are available in a wide range of sizes and colors.

All the projects in this book specify the size endcap you'll need, but once you start experimenting, you'll need to figure that out on your own. It's easy to measure the diameter of the braid using calipers.

When measuring with calipers, it is important to avoid squeezing the braid too tightly or you'll get an inaccurate reading. Say you measure your braid and get a reading of 4.5mm. What does that mean? A 5mm endcap will be a perfect fit, a 6mm endcap will be a somewhat-loose-but-OK fit, and maybe you can squeeze it into a 4mm endcap if you're really determined and you bind the braid very tightly. When shopping for endcaps and cones, remember that the inside diameter is the measurement that matters. Some cones and endcaps are labeled with the outside diameter.

Endcap Sizing Cheat Sheet

Braiding Fiber (one piece per warp)	Endcap Size
Size 8 pearl cotton	2mm
Vergata ribbon	3–4mm
Size 18 nylon string	3–4mm
1mm satin cord	5–6mm
2mm satin cord	6mm

Fiber-Focused
Braiding

Basic Braid Set

This braid is known as *kongo gumi* in Japanese, which means "strong braid." It's often referred to as the Basic Round Braid or Spiral Braid. It's the most common braid used for jewelry and the easiest to learn—in fact, every project in this book uses the basic movements you're about to learn. After working through this project, you'll have a beautiful necklace, a bracelet, and a great foundation for the rest of our kumihimo adventure.

Finished braid length: approximately 27"
Finished necklace length: up to 20" (including endcaps and clasp)
Finished bracelet length: up to 9" (including endcaps and clasp)

YOU'LL NEED

- Basic Kumihimo Toolkit

- 12 yd. 1mm satin cord
  (6 yd. each of two different colors)

- Pendant with 6mm or larger bail

- 4 6mm endcaps with loops

- 2 clasps

- 4 jump rings (4mm ID)

Setup

We'll set up two colors to make a spiraling stripe pattern. Cut eight 1.5-yd. pieces (four each of two colors). Bring the eight ends together so they're more or less even **[A]**. Don't worry about this too much. Tie all eight cords together using an overhand knot: Make a loop and bring the tails through the loop **[B]**. Make the knot fairly close to the end of the cords. I find it easiest to make a large loop and walk the knot toward the end of the cords rather than trying to make a small loop and knot right near the end.

Look at your disk and notice the four black dots. (If you're working on the blank side, take a pen and transfer the dots from the front.) These are there to help us evenly space the cords during Setup.

TIP When reading kumihimo patterns, the top position (farthest from your body) is called North. The bottom position (closest to your body) is called South. Left is West and Right is East.

Position the knot so that it's in the middle of the hole in the disk **[C]**. Now pick a cord—any cord. Lock it in one of the slots adjacent to the top dot. It doesn't matter which side of the dot. If your disk is brand new, it may take a little *umpf* to get it secured. Now take a cord the same color as the first and lock it in the slot on the other side of the top dot. That's one per slot—no sharing.

SATIN CORD

Satin cord usually comes on a spool or coiled. If you're working from a spool, the easiest way to proceed is to measure and cut one piece and then simply cut the others to match. In bead stores, rattail is often sold in 6-yd. coils. If you cut the six yards into four equal pieces, you will get 1½-yd. lengths without having to measure.

The easiest way to handle it is to keep it coiled as you remove it from the package. Drape the coil over a finger or thumb of one hand and use your other hand to hold the end of the cord as you unwind the coil. Bring the ends together to fold the piece in half. If you were to cut the folded end, you'd get two equal pieces. You want four equal pieces, so fold the piece in half one more time. Before you cut the ends, check if the folded pieces are about a hand-to-hand length (remember that we're shooting for 1½ yd.). If the cord is significantly shorter, you've folded too many times.

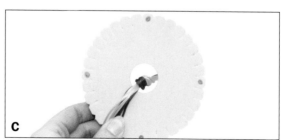

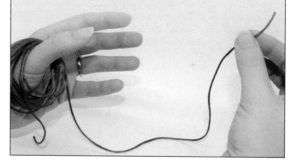

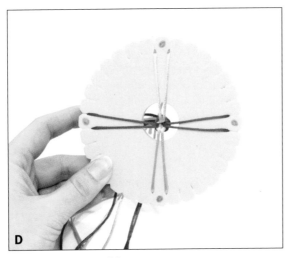

D

Standard starting position

Working again with the same color, lock one cord on each side of the bottom dot. Now you have two dots and four cords remaining. You get three guesses where they go—that's right. Lock a cord on each side of the left and right dots **[D]**. Your colors should be in matching pairs with one color in the North and South positions and another color in the East and West positions. It doesn't matter if the cords are somewhat jumbled. Anything you don't like at the beginning of the braid can be cut off when we finish.

Double check your work: Each of the eight cords should be firmly locked into a slot. One pair of cords should straddle each of the four dots, with the cords flush against the disk's surface. The knot should be centered in the hole and flush with the surface also. Perfect! This is the *standard starting position*. The arrangement of the colors will vary with other projects, but when I tell you to put the cords (I also refer to them as *warps*) on the disk in the standard starting position, this is what I'm talking about.

E

With these loose long ends, you have a tangled mess waiting to happen. Bobbins to the rescue! Open a bobbin by gently bending the domed side out. Use your thumb to hold a cord end against the core of the bobbin **[E]**. With your other hand, wind the cord onto the bobbin. It doesn't matter if you wind toward you or away from you.

Wind until the bobbin is about 1" below the disk, then pop the bobbin closed. As you braid, you'll discover the ideal length for you; in general, the shorter you keep the cords, the less they spin around and tangle. Wind each of the eight cords onto a bobbin **[F]**.

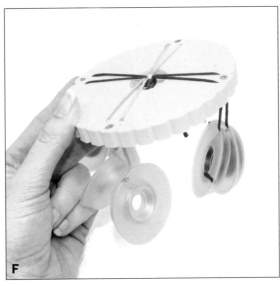

F

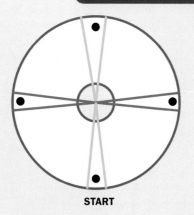

START

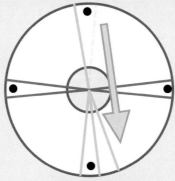

TOP-RIGHT DOWN

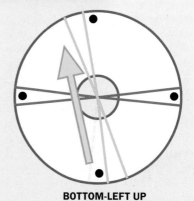

BOTTOM-LEFT UP

STOPPING POINT!
Whenever you need to take a break or pause for any reason, do so with three cords at the bottom.

Top-right down. Bottom-left up. That's it. Two moves. Things to know: The top of the disk is the side farthest from your body. The bottom of the disk is the side closest to your body. You're on your own for keeping left and right straight.

Ready? Let's do it together. Lift the top-right cord out of its slot. Bring it straight down to the bottom-right slot and lock it next to the two cords that are already at the bottom. Remember: one warp per slot; no sharing. Notice that it starts on the right and finishes on the right. This is important. Cords in this braid only move vertically (straight up and down)—never side to side or diagonally.

Observe that you now have one cord at the top and three at the bottom. This is our **stopping point**. Go ahead and set the disk down. You can come back to it later and always know where you left off if you stop at a stopping point. Ringing phone? Come to a stopping point before you answer. Want to take a break? Stopping point. Need to refer back to the book? Stopping point. If you don't stop at a stopping point, you have four pairs of cords evenly spaced and you have to figure out where you left off. I'll explain how to figure that out later, but for now, let's develop good habits by always stopping at a stopping point.

Break's over. From the stopping point, our next move is bottom-left up. Lift the bottom-left cord out of its slot. Bring it straight up to the top-left position and lock it in the slot next to the one cord already there. Again the rule is one warp per slot. Make sure that this left-side cord stays on the left and doesn't mistakenly get placed on the right. Many people find it helpful to use the right hand

for right-side moves and the left hand for left-side moves. This can help prevent accidently crossing the cords.

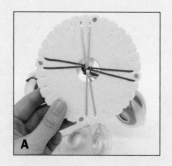

So far, so good. It may seem like you haven't really done anything, but notice how the cords you moved are no longer straddling the dots **[A]**. Remember that the dots are used just for setup. Now that you're braiding, you can ignore them. Time to turn the disk. Turn the disk a quarter turn so that the other color is at the top **[B]**. It doesn't matter which way you turn: Clockwise or counterclockwise is up to you. Using a consistent rotation will help you when you learn more-complicated braids, but for this braid it doesn't matter. The braid is round and the moves are symmetrical, so if you turn clockwise for a while and then start turning counterclockwise, it won't make any difference at all. Isn't it nice knowing that

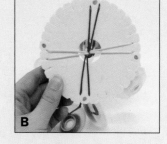

this is one less thing to worry about? Just turn the disk.

Now repeat the sequence a few hundred times and you'll be done before you know it: Top-right down. Bottom-left up. Turn.

21

I forgot to stop at a stopping point. Now what?

No problem. Just take a look at the middle of the braid where the eight warps meet, also known as the point of braiding. There should be two warps on top. By that I mean they are physically on top of the pile. Those two warps just moved. If you find these warps in the vertical position, you moved them but haven't turned the disk yet. Turn the disk and move the top-right cord down. If the warps that just moved are in the horizontal position, you moved them and turned the disk. Move the top-right warp down.

You need to turn the disk. This is the correct point of braiding.

You're pulling too hard!

How do I know if my tension is OK?

For the most part, the foam disk does a great job of managing tension for you. As long as the braid stays mostly in the middle of the hole and isn't jerking side to side with every move, your tension is just fine. If the braid is moving around, try easing up a bit on the tension. If the warps are falling out of the slots, then the tension is too loose.

Even tension comes with practice. In the beginning, most people tend to pull harder on one side than the other. Be conscious of your movements, relax, and with time it will even out.

This doesn't look right. I think I made a mistake.

First of all, take a deep breath. It's going to be all right. If you have a mistake in your braid, you have a couple of options. First of all, you can ignore it. This is an especially appealing option if you're near the beginning or end of the braid. Any oopsies can always be cut off if your braid is long enough. If that's your choice, keep on braiding. If necessary, shift the warps so that they're back to the starting position.

The second approach to dealing with a braiding error is to undo it and fix it. Unbraiding is just like braiding, except all of the moves are in reverse and it takes a lot more concentration. (Turn the TV off for this part.)

Start by identifying where you left off. Since we're dealing with a braiding error, the point of braiding might not look exactly like the photo in the previous section, but you're still looking for which one or two warps are on top of the pile. Now that you know where you are, you're going to unbraid one warp at a time. **Warning! Do not move more than one warp at a time. Do not take all of the warps off the disk and start moving them around randomly.**

The reverse braiding moves are: top-left down, bottom-right up, turn.

Pay close attention while unbraiding. You're looking for the mistake so you can correct it.

22

Crossover

Crossing a warp from side to side in addition to up and down is by far the most common mistake [A]. Remember that a warp that starts on the right finishes on the right. A warp that starts on the left finishes on the left. Crossover usually happens when, instead of moving the bottom-left warp straight up to the top-left, you move it up, cross it over the warp that's there, and place it in the top-right slot [B]. Even if your topmost warps don't contain a crossover, if you notice that pairs of warps are not evenly spaced, you probably have one or more crossovers farther back in the braid [C]. Just braid backward until you find the crossover and then correct the mistake.

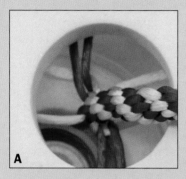

A

B

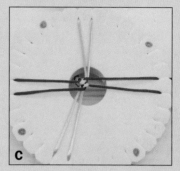

C

Wrong move after a stopping point

There are only two correct layouts for the warps. After fully completing a sequence they should be arranged 2, 2, 2, 2 around the disk. This is also the starting position for the braid. At a stopping point, which is halfway through the sequence, they are 1, 2, 3, 2 (clockwise around the disk starting at the top). If you ever have more than one group of three warps, you have a problem. That might look like 1, 3, 3, 1. What happened is that you were at a stopping point and therefore had a group of three warps at the bottom of the disk. The next correct move was bottom-left up, turn; however, in this case you skipped bottom-left up and turned the disk without completing the sequence.

Moving warps out of turn

After completing the top-right down, bottom-left up (but before rotating), the vertical warps should be in two parallel lines. If the top half seems slightly skewed—shifted sideways—you forgot to rotate and did top-right down, bottom-left up twice in a row on the same axis. Just unbraid the last moves, rotate, and continue.

FINISHING

Taking the braid off the disk

You're nearing the end. Some or all of the bobbins have probably fallen off by now. Even if the braid looks long enough for your project, at this point you may as well use up all of the fiber. We'll cut the braid to the perfect length and any scrap braid can be added to your kumihimo notebook. Just keep braiding until one warp is too short to lock into a slot on the disk. Note: One warp always finishes before the others, no matter how evenly you cut them at the beginning and even if your tension was perfect. One always comes up shorter than the rest. That's life. Don't sweat it.

Now that you're finished braiding, remove any remaining bobbins. Holding the braid right below the disk **[A]**, remove each of the eight warps from its slot. Tie all eight cords together using an overhand knot—just like at the beginning of the braid.

At this point the braid may look a little thicker and stiffer than anticipated. Here's why: We haven't relaxed it yet. Take hold of the braid at either end and pull in opposite directions. You'll notice that the braid gets longer, thinner, and softer. Pretty neat, huh? Once you've relaxed the braid, you shouldn't experience any further stretching unless you're braiding with a stretchy fiber. The satin cord is good about holding its shape once relaxed, but

you'll find that some yarns (especially if you have a heavy pendant) just keep stretching forever.

Binding

You now have a beautiful made-by-you kumihimo braid, but it's not a necklace yet. To make that transformation we need to add our endcaps, but first we have to do something about the huge knot at either end of the braid. You know what's coming, don't you? We're going to have to cut the braid. Don't panic! I'll walk you through binding each end of the braid so it doesn't unravel when you cut.

Now is a good time to have a look at the beginning of the braid. Any mistakes near the start you'd like to cut off? Is it just somewhat funny-looking near the knot? You decide where to place the binding. If your braid is perfectly perfect in every way right from the start, wow! Good for you! You still can't bind too close to the knot. Be sure to leave enough room to get the scissors in.

Cut a piece of binding thread about 18" long. Fold it over so it's not quite in half. You want a long side and a short side. By folding it over you've created a loop of thread. It's not twisted or wrapped or anything, but this little U-turn in the thread is our loop. Place the loop on top of and parallel to the braid wherever you would like the binding to be **[B]**.

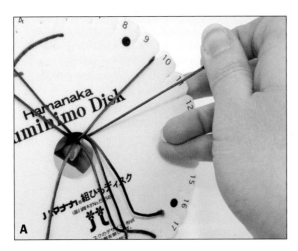

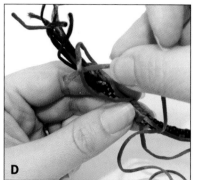

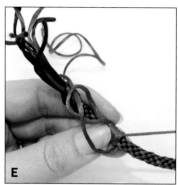

In photos B–D, I used satin cord because it's easier to see. You should use beading thread for binding. Photos F and G show what a binding will look like when you use beading thread.

At this point, I usually hold the braid in my nondominant hand. I'm right-handed, so the knot is on the left and I hold the loop in place, just to the right of the knot, in my left hand. Use your dominant hand to wrap the longer piece of thread around the braid [C]. The short piece of thread is on top of the braid, so it gets covered by the wraps as well.

Take your time with this and make it neat. You want each wrap to lie next to—not on top of—the wrap before. Keep it snug. You want to make about five to seven wraps. If you prefer not to count, the wraps should be between ⅛" and ¼" wide.

Remember when we talked about maybe squeezing a braid into a smaller endcap? If that's part of your plan, do the squeezing during the binding by wrapping extra tight. Keep holding everything with your nondominant hand, and use your dominant hand to bring the working thread through the loop [D]. (The working thread started as the longer piece, but it is shorter now because we've been wrapping with it.) Grab the short tail (it's just been hanging out this whole time) and pull [E]. Pulling the short tail closes the loop. Ta da!

Pull the threads in opposite directions to tighten everything up. Make an extra little square knot on top for good measure [F]. Trim the thread tails as close as you can, but don't cut the braid yet.

You decided at the beginning how long you want your necklace to be. Now is the time to put that magic number to use. For example, I like my necklaces 17" long. I've already picked out my endcaps and clasp and I know that my findings will add 1". That means that I need to cut the braid 16" long. Measuring from my first binding near the beginning of the braid, I make a second bind 16" down the braid. A half-inch down from there I bind again. This is the start of my bracelet. I like my bracelets 6½" long, and I'm going to use the same endcaps and clasp as for the necklace, so I subtract 1" from my desired length and make my second bracelet binding 5½" from the start of the bracelet. There's still a usable length of braid after I measure for my bracelet, so I make another binding ½" down. Note that whenever you want to cut the braid into two usable pieces, you need to make two bindings and cut between them [G].

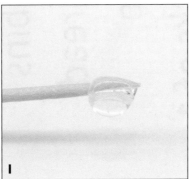

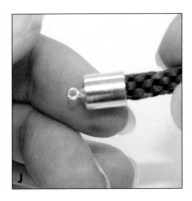

Cutting

Before you cut a cord, it's important to gather all of the materials and tools you'll need for gluing. The little binding that you made in the last step isn't really attached to the braid. If you cut the end off and then toss the braid in your "to be finished later" drawer (we all have one), the binding can walk right off the end of the braid.

Look at the bindings. Notice that for every binding there is a "keep" side and a "throw away" side. Be sure to cut on the "throw away" side or you'll cut the binding off. Using your best scissors, cut as close to the binding as possible without cutting through the binding itself **[H]**. The most important thing about cutting is to be brave. One cut. No hacking. No haircuts. Do this for each end of the necklace and bracelet.

Leave it alone! No haircuts!

Adding a pendant

Some pendants have bails large enough to fit over the endcap; others don't. Find out before you glue the endcaps on. If the bail is too small to fit over the endcap, add the pendant after cutting off the knot but before gluing on the endcap. If it's going to be a really tight squeeze getting the pendant onto the braid, consider smearing a tiny tab of glue onto the binding and letting it dry before putting the pendant on. This way the friction from the pendant doesn't pull the binding off.

Gluing

I work over a small scrap of paper so I don't get glue on the table. Open the E6000 and squeeze a small blob (yes, that's the technical term) onto a toothpick **[I]**. Use the toothpick to smear the glue around the inside of the endcap. Cover the bottom and sides of the endcap so that it's about half-full of glue. Hold the braid still with one hand and use the other hand to slowly twist and push the endcap onto the braid **[J]**. The more slowly you push, the more time the glue has to soak into the braid, resulting in less excess glue oozing from the endcap. If you encounter an ooze situation, use a clean toothpick to wipe the excess glue away. If you do this right away, you'll notice that the glue balls up like rubber cement and is very easy to remove. Some styles of endcaps have a little hole near the ring. If so, be sure to check this area for ooze too.

Now comes the hardest part: waiting. After you have glued endcaps to each end of the necklace and bracelet, set everything aside to dry overnight.

Attaching a clasp

Now that the glue has dried, you can use jump rings to attach the clasp of your choice. Remember that when opening and closing jump rings, you hold one side of the ring steady and push the other side away from or toward you **[K]**. Never pull the ends straight out to the side. Open a jump ring, slide on any loops or half of the clasp **[L]**, and close the jump ring.

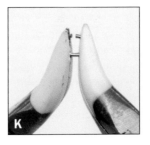

Playing with Color

Now that you have the basic moves down, it's time to start playing with color. Think of all the possibilities for custom-colored braids. The last project used two colors, but an eight-warp braid could use up to eight different colors. What would that look like? What about three or four colors?

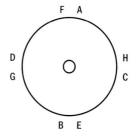

Disk setup

The color pattern is determined by how the colors are arranged at the start of the braid. So how do you know which setup to use to get the color pattern you want?

Follow a pattern from a book. Every project in this book has a starting diagram showing the initial arrangement of colors. Copy it exactly or substitute your own color choices. If you keep the color ratio and placement the same, you'll get the same pattern in your braid.

Keep a kumihimo notebook. When you start a new project, take note of the starting position of each color. It's also helpful to jot down what fiber you used and how long you cut each warp. When you're finished braiding, add a photo of the necklace or a scrap of braid. This way if you find a pattern you really like, you can remember how you did it. Conversely, if you create a braid that you don't like, you can avoid repeating it.

Make a photocopy of the braid diagram on this page and color in your own design. Just remember that every block of the same letter has to be the same color. For example, if you choose red for the "A" warp, all of the blocks labeled "A" need to be colored in red.

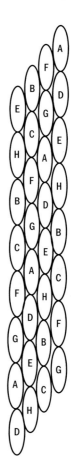

Braid diagram

A few of the most popular color patterns

Two Colors—Stripes

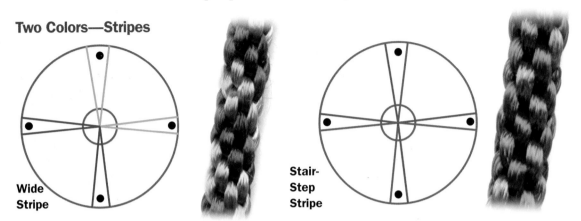

Wide Stripe

Stair-Step Stripe

Two Colors—Polka Dots

Three Colors

Four Colors

Five Colors

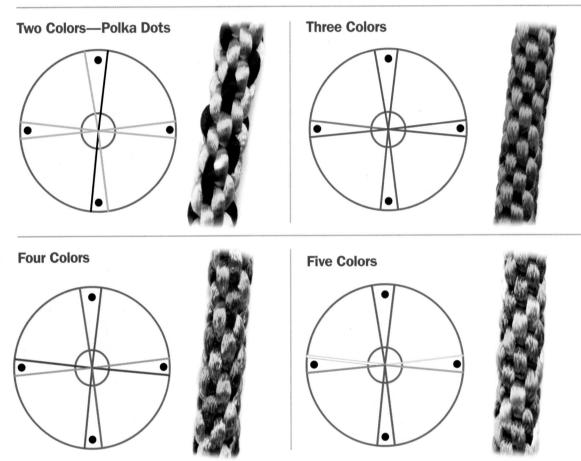

Variegated Fiber

You have two options when it comes to variegated fibers: Just let the colors fall where they may, or match up the repeats so the colors change in unison, as I did in this piece.

Autumn

Vergata is a thin, flat tube ribbon that comes in variegated colors. I don't usually bother matching the repeats in variegated fibers because I like how the colors blend and shift organically. Just cut the cords and let the colors fall where they may. The shifting colors—tan and cream into brown and black, copper into burnt sienna—are reminiscent of the changing autumn leaves.

Finished length: 16½" (double strand, including clasp)

29

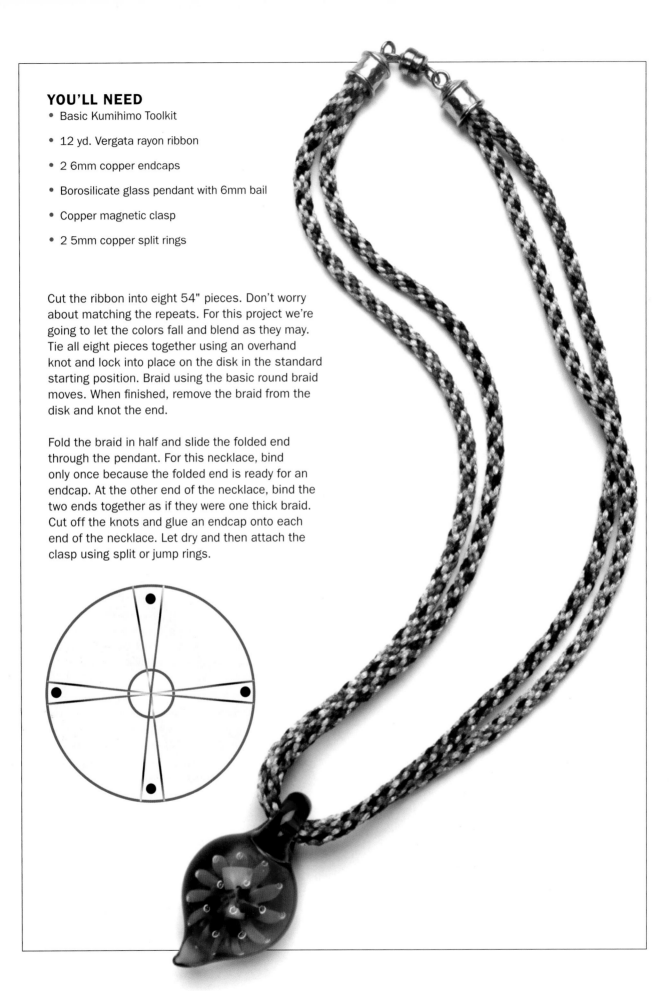

YOU'LL NEED

- Basic Kumihimo Toolkit

- 12 yd. Vergata rayon ribbon

- 2 6mm copper endcaps

- Borosilicate glass pendant with 6mm bail

- Copper magnetic clasp

- 2 5mm copper split rings

Cut the ribbon into eight 54" pieces. Don't worry about matching the repeats. For this project we're going to let the colors fall and blend as they may. Tie all eight pieces together using an overhand knot and lock into place on the disk in the standard starting position. Braid using the basic round braid moves. When finished, remove the braid from the disk and knot the end.

Fold the braid in half and slide the folded end through the pendant. For this necklace, bind only once because the folded end is ready for an endcap. At the other end of the necklace, bind the two ends together as if they were one thick braid. Cut off the knots and glue an endcap onto each end of the necklace. Let dry and then attach the clasp using split or jump rings.

Signature Necklace

Start with a kumihimo braid and select the beads
to match, or start with beads you love and make a
coordinating braid—it's up to you.

Finished length: approximately 20" (including clasp)

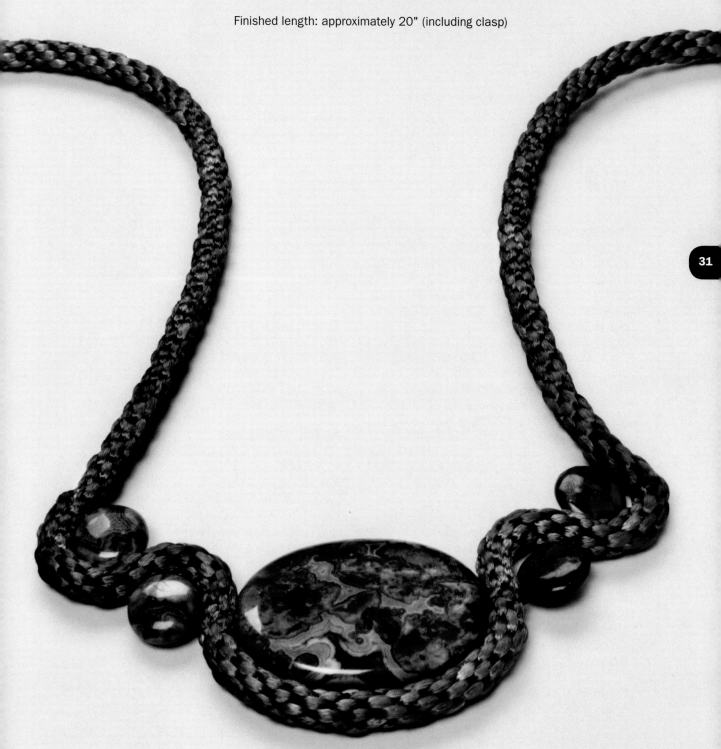

YOU'LL NEED
- Basic Kumihimo Toolkit

- Sewing pins with ball tips

- 24"–27" kumihimo braid made with 1mm or 2mm satin cord (I used 2mm hand-dyed satin; remove the braid from the disk and knot it at each end— don't bind or cut)

- 30x40mm flat oval bead

- 4 10–12mm coin beads

- Pair of 6mm magnetic endcaps

- Beading thread to match the color of the braid (I used One-G)

- Big Eye needle

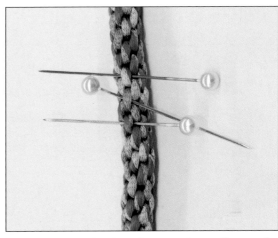

The three sewing pins show the mountains you'll sew under when making the figure-8 thread anchor.

You have flexibility with what type of beads you use for this project, but make sure they're drilled end to end (not front to back). I usually prefer flat coins and ovals, but some round beads could work as well. Just think about how they'll sit in relation to the braid. This necklace is all about the curve, so skip square or angular beads.

You don't have to follow my plan exactly. Think of all the wonderful, graceful lines you can draw with your braid. Take some time to plan out how you would like your necklace to look. Follow the shape of the focal bead. I like to hold the braid against the stones and shape it different ways. If you prefer, you could try pinning the braid to a cork board to test out different shapes.

Assembly
Did you know that you can sew beads directly to your kumihimo braid? The braid is really just a thick piece of fabric. The trick is hiding the thread path inside the braid.

Take a close look at a finished satin braid. Notice how the braid is made up of a pattern of rising and falling cords. I think of the highest point as a mountain and the lowest point as a valley. We're going to hide our thread under the mountains.

Before we start, let's take a closer look at the thread path. Pick up a pin. Starting in a valley,

pass the tip of the pin under a mountain and out the valley on the other side. Be sure that the pin is traveling under the mountain and not through it. You don't want to pierce a cord with the needle; you're just moving underneath a cord.

It's best to start in the middle of the braid with the focal bead and work out from there. The most important technique of this project is the figure-8 thread anchor. You'll use this to anchor the thread to the braid first and then to anchor the beads to the braid.

Figure-8 thread anchor
Cut a 2-yd. piece of One-G and thread a Big Eye needle near one end. Two mountains above the point where you want the first hole of the center bead to sit, sew under a mountain and pull the thread, leaving a 1-yd. tail **[A]** and **[C, a–b]**. Move to the next mountain in the same vertical line and sew under it going the opposite direction **[b–c]**. The thread should fall between the valley and the next row of mountains. Sew under the first mountain in the same direction as the first time **[c–d]**.

Now that you've made a circle, the thread should stay in place a bit better, but don't pull too hard yet. Sew under the second mountain in the same direction as before **[d–e]**. Note that each mountain has its own consistent direction of thread travel.

Move to the next mountain in the line and sew under it, moving in the opposite direction **[e–f]**. Sew under the second mountain again **[f–g]**. This completes the figure-8. Pull hard on the thread. It shouldn't pull out. If it does, reinforce. From this point on, it is important to tighten the thread after every move. Move the thread into place by sewing under mountains, being sure to always enter and exit the braid in a valley.

Holding the braid and the focal bead in the desired position, sew through the bead and under a mountain directly opposite the mountain you exited **[B] and [g–h]**. Repeat the figure-8 anchor on the opposite side of the bead. Reinforce by sewing back and forth through the bead. You don't necessarily have to do a figure-8 every time, but at least sew in a circle when you make a U-turn in the braid so the thread doesn't pull out.

After the focal bead is secure, add beads to either side using the same technique. To help keep things even, consider alternating the side you work on.

Tie off the thread with a half-hitch knot around a previous stitch (not around a mountain). Trim the tails as close as possible. Measure the width of the center section. Subtract that from your desired length and divide by two. Measure that distance from either side of the center section—that is where you should bind and cut the braid. Attach an endcap as usual.

A

B

C

No-Knot Start

By now you may have noticed that a big knot at each end of the braid gets cut off and thrown away. Tying eight cords together is a quick and easy way to get started on a project but it also creates waste, so I'm going to teach you a way to save fiber at the beginning of a braid: the "No-Knot Start."

Instead of cutting eight warps, cut four warps twice as long. For example, all of the previous projects called for 12 yd. of cord cut into eight 1½-yd. pieces. For a no-knot start, use 12 yd. of cord cut into four 3-yd. pieces.

Hold the four cords together so that the ends are lined up evenly. Fold the cords in half to find the middle. Using a scrap of thread, tie a knot around the middle point of the cords. Holding the tied middle point over the hole in the kumihimo disk, lock the cords in place in the standard starting position. Ta da! From four cords, you now have eight warps.

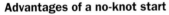

I like to position the North/South warps first and then the East/West warps. This way when I make the first top-right down move, the cord that I'm moving crosses over the East/West warps, creating a tidy start. Wind each warp onto a bobbin and braid as usual. Note that this trick works only for the start of the braid.

Advantages of a no-knot start
Less waste: Some fibers, like leather and silk, can be pricey. A no-knot start saves inches.

Maximize your material: Sometimes you don't have as much of a fiber as you want or it comes in a precut length.

Incorporate a finding directly into a braid: This works for findings such as rings and large loops.

You'll learn how to do all of these things in the key chain project that follows.

TECHNIQUES: NO-KNOT START, FINISHING WITH A TASSEL, WIRE-WRAPPING

Suede Leather Key Chain

In some cases it's handy to incorporate a finding before starting to braid. In this project, you'll string a large jump ring onto the cords before you begin locking them into place onto the disk, and it will become an integral part of the braid.

Finished length: 6½" (including 3" tassel)

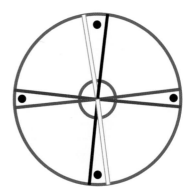

YOU'LL NEED
- Basic Kumihimo Toolkit
- Flush cutters
- 8 ft. ⅛"-wide deerskin suede leather lace (2 ft. each of four different colors)
- 7–8mm inside diameter soldered jump ring
- 6" 22-gauge craft wire in a coordinating color
- 1"-diameter key ring

Working with suede leather
Suede lace is flat with a shiny side and a fuzzy side. I tend to let it twist around while braiding, but if you were so inclined, you could carefully arrange the suede at the start of the braid so that each warp is facing the same direction (all fuzzy side up, for example). Then every time you move a warp, you would be sure to fold it across the disk so that the alternate side is then facing up. In this way the braid gets an orderly pattern of fuzzy, shiny, fuzzy, shiny. Like I said, I don't bother with this level of detail and just enjoy the random texture.

Setup
Hold the four suede pieces together so the ends line up evenly. Fold the suede in half to find the middle. Using a small scrap of thread, tie a knot around the midpoint of the suede. String the jump ring onto all four suede pieces so it sits on the thread knot **[A]**. Holding the tied midpoint and jump ring over the hole in the kumihimo disk, lock the cords in place using the standard starting position **[B]**.

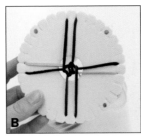

Braid using the basic round braid moves. Keep an eye on the length; don't braid all the way to the end of the warps because we're making a tassel.

This braid will look very fat coming out of the disk. Relax the braid by pinching it right below the disk and pulling on the ring. When the braid is 3" long

(relaxed length), remove the braid from the disk and loosely knot the tails. Do not bind or cut.

Assembly
Trim the thread knot you made at the very beginning (near the jump ring) and remove the thread. Cut a 6" piece of craft wire and make a 90-degree bend about an inch from one end. This is our handle. Place the handle on top of the braid at the point just before the braid meets the tassel. The handle should be parallel to the braid. Hold the wire handle firmly in place using flatnose or chainnose pliers **[C]**.

Wrap the wire around the braid, pulling as tightly and as evenly as possible. Make three to four wraps, each one snug next to the one before. Use the flush cutters to snip the wire close to the braid **[D]**. Attach the key ring to the jump ring. Untie the tails. This is the tassel. You can leave it as is or give it a haircut. I measured 3" from the wire binding and cut through all eight suede pieces at once so they'd be even.

KUMIHIMO MATH

The goal for this key chain is a 3" braid with a 3" tassel. Use the three-to-one rule for the braid: three times three is nine. Then add 3" for the tassel. That gives us 12". Doubled for the no-knot start, that equals 24", so cut four pieces of suede 24" each.

Combining Fibers

In the projects so far, each warp has been only a single cord, but a warp can also be made up of several threads or cords. In fact, in traditional Japanese kumihimo, each warp is composed of many fine pieces of silk thread: One thread alone is too thin to be a warp and the resulting braid would be uselessly tiny, but the bundled silk threads have an appropriate thickness.

In the Twisted Spiral Braid, half of the warps are single 1mm satin cords and half are bundles of three 1mm satin cords. Why not just use 3mm satin cord? Because this way we can make custom color blends. I combined olive green and antique gold on one warp to create a color of 3mm satin cord that isn't commercially available.

Another reason to combine multiple fibers per warp is so thinner fibers can be carried by thicker ones. In the Metallic Twist Necklace, each warp is composed of one thin piece of metallic thread and one piece of satin cord. A single metallic thread alone as a warp would be too thin and would be swallowed by the thicker satin cord. Multiple pieces of metallic thread combined to make a thicker warp could overwhelm the necklace. By allowing the satin cord to carry the metallic thread, we'll strike a nice balance with just a touch of sparkle.

In both of these projects, the trick to getting the multiple fibers to act as one is to give the warp a gentle twist every time you move it. This helps prevent one fiber from separating from the others and creating a lump or loop in the braid. Be consistent in the direction of the twist.

I encourage you to play with this concept. Experiment with custom color combinations and textures.

Twisted Spiral Braid

A spiral pattern can be achieved with color alone, but if you combine different thicknesses, a spiral becomes a lovely textural element.

Finished length: 20"

38

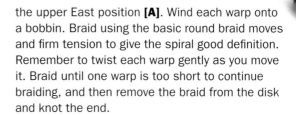

YOU'LL NEED

- Basic Kumihimo Toolkit

- 6 yd. medium brown 1mm satin cord (cut into 4 1½-yd. pieces)

- 16½ yd. olive green 1mm satin cord (cut into 11 1½-yd. pieces)

- 1½ yd. antique gold 1mm satin cord

- Enameled copper pendant with 11mm copper bail

- 2 10mm enameled copper cones

- 2 2" copper headpins

- Copper magnetic clasp

- 2 3mm copper jump rings

Setup

Tie all 16 pieces of satin cord together using an overhand knot. Lock the cords on the disk using the following arrangement: a medium brown cord in each of the West and South positions, three olive green cords in both of the North positions, three olive green cords in the lower East position, and two olive green cords and an antique gold cord in the upper East position [A]. Wind each warp onto a bobbin. Braid using the basic round braid moves and firm tension to give the spiral good definition. Remember to twist each warp gently as you move it. Braid until one warp is too short to continue braiding, and then remove the braid from the disk and knot the end.

Wire-wrapping the cones

Feed a headpin up through the cone so the pin extends from the small hole. With the tip of your chainnose pliers, grasp the wire directly above the cone. Bend the wire (above the pliers) into a right angle [B]. Using roundnose pliers, position the jaws in the bend and bring the wire over the top jaw of the pliers [C]. Reposition the lower jaw snugly in the loop. Curve the wire downward around the bottom jaw of the pliers [D]. Position the bent chainnose pliers' jaws across the loop and wrap the wire around the wire stem, covering the stem between the loop and the cone [E]. Trim the excess wire and press the cut end close to the wraps with chainnose pliers. Now this cone is an endcap! Repeat for the second cone.

Assembly

Bind and cut the braid to your desired length. Slide the pendant onto the middle of the braid. Glue a wire-wrapped cone to each end.

> **TIP** The cones I chose for this project had decorative holes on the sides. If using a similar style, be extra careful to check for ooze before setting them aside to dry.

Allow to dry overnight. Attach the magnetic clasp using jump rings.

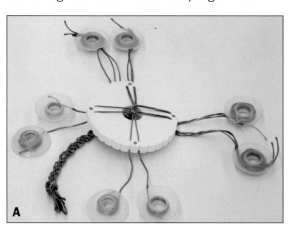

A

B

C

D

E

Metallic Twist

My eye is really drawn to the dichroic glass in the seashell pendant, and I wanted to bring some of that glitter into the braid. For the metallic twist, we'll add a bit of sparkle by incorporating silver and gold metallic thread into the braid.

Finished length: 18" (including clasp)

YOU'LL NEED

- Basic Kumihimo Toolkit

- 12 yd. 1mm black satin cord

- 6 yd. silver metallic thread

- 6 yd. gold metallic thread

- Borosilicate glass shell pendant with 6mm bail

- 2 6mm (inside diameter) hammered-texture pewter cones

- Hammered-texture pewter clasp

- 2 2" headpins

- 2 4x6mm oval jump rings

Setup

For this braid, each warp will contain one piece of black satin cord and one piece of metallic thread. Cut eight 54" pieces of black rattail, four 54" pieces of silver metallic thread, and four 54" pieces of gold metallic thread.

Tie all 16 pieces together using an overhand knot. Using the standard starting position, lock the black and silver warps in the North and South positions and the black and gold warps in the East and West positions **[A]**.

Braid using the basic round braid moves, giving each warp a little twist as you move it across the disk. It doesn't matter which direction you twist, as long as you are consistent **[B]**.

When finished braiding, remove the braid from the disk and tie an overhand knot at the end. Wire-wrap both cones. Bind and cut the braid to the desired length (the cones and toggle will add about 2"). Gently slide the pendant to the middle of the necklace.

Glue on the cones and let dry overnight.

Attach the clasp using jump rings.

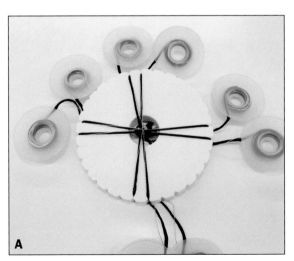

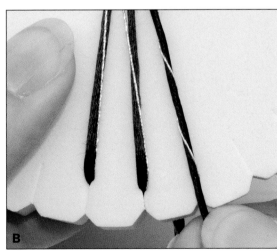

Braiding
with Beads

Braiding with Beads

When I made my first kumihimo bracelet, my first thought after "Well, that was neat!" was "How can I add beads?" If you too are approaching kumihimo as a beader, you've probably been asking that same question from page 1.

BEADED KUMIHIMO TOOLKIT

Braiding with beads is a lot like making a fiber-focused braid. The moves are the same and we need only a few additions to the toolkit; what varies is the type of stringing material and beads. Setup for beaded kumihimo remains constant for all projects: Cut the cords, tie them together, and lock them on the disk. String beads on each warp and wind each beaded cord on a bobbin.

Start with everything in the basic toolkit and add weighted bobbins, a centerweight, a Big Eye needle, a fuzzy beading mat, a bead spinner, and a bead spinner needle. A resting stand is optional.

Weighted bobbins

I mentioned earlier that you wouldn't need weights until you started working with beads. The reason is that the foam disk does a pretty good job of gripping the cords as long as they're at least 1mm in diameter—thinner than that and they start slipping and sliding.

For most of our beaded projects, we'll work with thin threads; by using weighted bobbins, you give some heft to the bobbins, and gravity will help hold everything in place. You can easily make these bobbins yourself (see mini project on the next page) or look for bobbins based on my design made by BeadSmith.

Centerweight

Having downward tension in the braid makes it easier to keep your beads in place, so I always use a centerweight in addition to the weighted bobbins. Originally I used a pair of crosslocking tweezers as my weight, but I've grown fond of a product known as Gatorweights, cylindrical steel weights with an attached alligator clip. They're available in two weights, regular and light, and I like them both, but the Gatorweight Lite is my most-used weight. For all projects in this book, use a Gatorweight Lite as a centerweight unless otherwise specified.

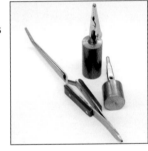

Sometimes I switch to the lighter crosslocking tweezers when I'm braiding with large (4mm+) beads. For tiny seed beads (11° and smaller), I like the heavier Gatorweight. Some students use hemostat clamps or bags of pennies. It's a matter of personal preference, but keep in mind that a heavier weight makes a looser braid.

Wait a minute. Shouldn't a heavier weight make my braid tighter? Let's think about what the centerweight is doing to the braid. It's pulling the point of braiding down through the hole. The lower the point of braiding, the more thread is used with every move. Using more thread each move results in a longer stitch and a looser braid. A looser braid also means that more of the thread is showing.

Some students ask if they really need to use the weighted bobbins and centerweight. It's certainly possible to braid with beads without using weights. That's how I did my first few beaded braids. Without weights it's trickier to get the beads into the correct position in the braid and, once there, the beads are more likely to escape. Everything is too light and wants to slip and slide around the disk. You really have to pay attention to what you're doing.

Weighted bobbins are the secret: Students opting to use weights learn the technique faster, have fewer escapee beads, and in general are most satisfied with their beaded braids.

Big Eye needle

The cord we load our beads onto is too thick to pass through the eye of a standard beading needle, so use a Big Eye needle. It's essentially two thin, flexible pieces of metal soldered together at each end, creating an eye that runs the entire length of the needle. Use a short tail when using a Big Eye needle, because the point where the cord is gripped by the needle will be weakened.

Bead spinner

When it comes to quickly stringing lots of beads, a bead spinner is the best invention since microwave popcorn! It harnesses the power of centrifugal force to push the spinning beads onto a curved needle. Like magic! Use the curved bead spinner needle that's often sold with the spinner; other needles won't work. Big-eye bead spinner needles are too floppy and they bend under the firm grip needed to control the bead spinner.

Seed beads

Seed beads are a great choice for beaded kumihimo. They come in an astounding array of colors and finishes. They're available in a variety of sizes from the teeny-tiny 15° to the still-pretty-small 6°. Choose round beads for a smooth braid or experiment with hexes or triangles for faceted flair.

Japanese seed beads are the most uniform in size and shape and are my favorite type of seed beads. I've also braided successfully with Czech seed beads, although they vary greatly in size. Some beads will be thick and tall while others are flat little donuts. You can either cull the odd beads at the beginning or just ignore the difference and enjoy the texture it brings to your project. Avoid Chinese seed beads; the holes tend to be roughly finished and can cut through the string.

Resting stand

When braiding with beads, you'll frequently need to readjust the length of string hanging out of the bobbins. I find it handy to use some sort of resting stand. I set my disk on top of a roll of paper towels or a heavy glass vase. The resting stand acts as a third hand for me when I need to open a bobbin to let down more string. Other options for resting stands include thick cardboard tubes, PVC pipe, or heavy drinking glasses. You'll still hold the disk in your hand when braiding; the resting stand is used only when you need to adjust the bobbins.

MINI PROJECT

Making weighted bobbins

YOU'LL NEED
- 8 plastic bobbins
- Coarse sandpaper (I use 50-grit)
- E6000 glue
- Toothpick
- 8 heavy washers*
  *I use USS Super 9 zinc washers; their 1/2"-diameter hole is a perfect fit on the plastic bobbins. Use sandpaper to really rough up one of the smooth sides of each bobbin. This helps the glue adhere.

Pop all of the bobbins into the open position. Spread a generous amount of glue onto a washer. Press the washer firmly to the roughed-up surface of the bobbin. Let dry overnight.

The roughed-up surface helps the washer adhere well to the bobbin.

You may be wondering how to figure out how many seed beads to use. The rule of thumb with seed beads when using the same size bead on all eight warps is: You need half your finished length in beads per warp. For example, if you're making an 18" beaded braid, you need 9" of beads on each of the eight warps. If you're making an 8" bracelet, you need 4" of beads on each warp.

If you're mixing sizes or not using beads on all warps, this rule won't hold true, but it's still a good starting point if you need to make an educated guess. Each project in this book tells you how many beads you need.

Other beads
You can braid with pretty much any type of small bead. I generally stick to 4mm or smaller for my main beads, but I go larger for focal beads as you'll see in the "Braiding with Teardrops" section.

Stringing material
With bead stitching techniques such as peyote stitch or herringbone stitch, thin thread gains strength with multiple passes through each bead. In kumihimo, the stringing material passes through each bead only once, so beading threads such as Nymo, One-G, or Silamide are unsuitably weak and thin. It's also important that the kumihimo stringing material fill as much of the bead hole as possible. In fact, our beaded kumihimo stringing material is more of a thin cord than thread.

Twisted nylon string
This is the string I use most often for beaded kumihimo. C-Lon and Superlon (S-Lon) are two common brands, and they're available in a few different thicknesses. I use the size 18 string with 8º or 6º seed beads. Go for the micro string if you're using 11ºs or 15ºs.

Pearl cotton
I like to use size 8 pearl cotton when I'm braiding with 11ºs. It fills the hole completely, resulting in a firm braid. (Note that some colors, especially silver-lined or color-lined, have a hard time fitting. You'll have to cull small-hole beads, so you may want to pick up an extra tube.) Most craft stores and knitting/crochet stores carry pearl cotton.

String color
Does the string color need to match the beads? It doesn't need to be an exact match, but try to keep them similar so the string blends into the background. On the other hand, maybe you'll choose hot pink string with your neon green beads as a design feature. It's up to you.

How much string do I need?
Use the same three-to-one rule we've been using for fiber-only kumihimo. That means for an 18" beaded braid, cut each warp 54" (1½ yd.) long. You'll have a fair amount of extra string, but the surplus helps keep the weighted bobbins from falling off and gives you the option of adding more beads and making a longer braid. Better to have warps too long than too short.

Length and fit
Beaded kumihimo necklaces can be quite thick—½–¾" in diameter. Allow about 15–20% extra length to ensure that the necklace fits the way you like. This is even more of an issue with bracelets because of the small circumference. The chunky Magatama Spiral is a little over ½" thick and about 9" long, but it fits a 7" wrist.

Size 18 string

Micro string

Beaded Rope

The Beaded Rope project teaches you the basics of braiding with beads. Use a large-hole art glass bead or a focal clasp to accent this classic beaded braid. The techniques learned in this project will be used for all future beaded kumihimo projects, so pay special attention to the setup and locking the beads into place.

Finished length: 18" (including clasp)

YOU'LL NEED

- Beaded Kumihimo Toolkit
- 12 yd. size 18 nylon string
- 30–35 grams 8º Japanese seed beads, single color or mix
- Cone finish: 2 25mm cones, 2 2" headpins, and 2 4mm oval jump rings
- Endcap finish: 8mm endcap set
- Clasp

TIP You'll have beads left over, but the bead spinner is easier to use when the bowl is full. You'll use about 20 grams.

Setup

Cut eight 1½-yd. pieces of nylon string, tie them together using an overhand knot, and lock them in place on the kumihimo disk in the standard starting position. To keep everything from tangling, wind all but one of the strings on a weighted bobbin. On the remaining warp, thread a Big Eye needle and string 8" of 8º seed beads by hand or by using a bead spinner (see below).

Tie a knot at the end of the string to keep the beads from falling off **[A]**. Push the beads together as a group toward the disk so that they are about 2" below it **[B]**.
Keep the beads together so they don't get tangled with the string. Starting at the loose end, wind the string and beads onto the bobbin **[C]**. Do this for each of the eight warps.

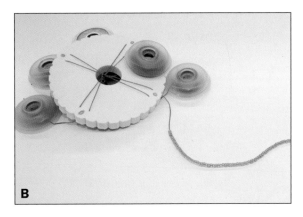

Bead spinner

Although using a bead spinner can be tricky at first, after you get the hang of it, you'll find it's a real time saver. To use a bead spinner, pour the seed beads into the bead spinner bowl. Cut a 6" piece of beading thread (not size 18 nylon; use the thin thread you use for binding). Thread the bead spinner needle. Tie the two ends of the thread together using an overhand knot; this loop of thin thread becomes the new eye of the needle. Unwind one bobbin. Thread the loose end of string through the thread eye of the bead spinner needle **[D]**.

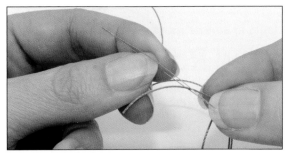

The eye of a **Big Eye** needle runs its entire length. The easiest way to open a new needle is to slide your thumbnail into the eye.

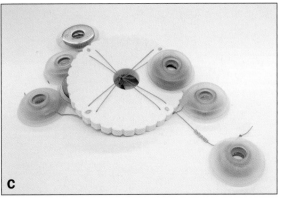

B

C

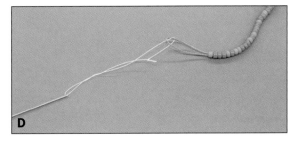

D

If you are right-handed, turn the bead spinner clockwise with your left hand and hold the needle with your right hand **[E]**. Left-handers should turn the bead spinner counterclockwise with the right hand, holding the needle with the left. Point the hook of the needle down and toward the outside of the bowl. Skim the surface of the beads. If you scrape the bottom, you won't pick up any beads.

Stop spinning after 1–3" of beads have climbed up the needle. Tip the needle so the beads slide over the thread eye and onto the string (you may have to give them a push). Spin and load beads until you have as many beads on the string as the project calls for. Tie a small knot at the end of the string to keep the beads from falling off.

This Beaded Rope necklace features a large-hole focal bead.

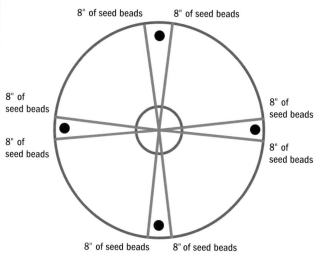

8" of seed beads 8" of seed beads

8" of seed beads

8" of seed beads

8" of seed beads

8" of seed beads

8" of seed beads 8" of seed beads

E

F

Check the setup
You have eight nylon-string warps tied together and locked on the disk. Each warp is strung with 8" of seed beads. At this point, all of the beads are below the disk. There's an inch or so of working thread (empty string) between the underside of the disk and the start of the beads. Clip the centerweight just below the knot **[F]**. Does your setup look like mine? Good.

Braid a nubbin without beads
Every beaded braid starts and ends with a short section without beads. This braided nubbin is where you'll bind and cut the braid. Using the standard top-right down, bottom-left up sequence, braid about ½" without adding any beads **[G]**.

G

49

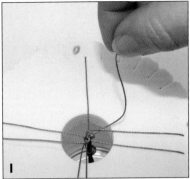

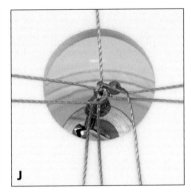

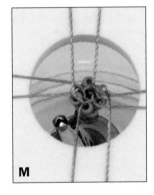

Braid with beads

The braiding sequence remains the same with or without beads: top-right down, bottom-left up. The only difference is that every time you move a warp, you slide one bead into the middle of the braid. I use my index finger to slide the bead forward while my other fingers hold the rest of the beads back **[H]**. Be sure to lock each bead into place by catching it under the first perpendicular warp that it crosses (cross-warp) **[I, J]**. The first four beads are tricky. Go slowly and give the warp plenty of slack as you move it.

When we catch the bead on the perpendicular warp, we're pulling the warp strings into the middle of the braid where they won't be visible.

Let's try it again. It's the same thing when doing the "bottom-left up" move: Give the string a lot of slack and gently tuck a bead under the first cross-warp **[K, L]**. The beads sit a little crookedly at first, but after the second round, the holes should be facing up and the beads should be arranged in a circle **[M]**. Keep an eye on the length of your working thread (the empty space between the bottom side of the disk and the start of the strung beads on the warp). When the beads are getting too close to the disk, come to a stopping point.

Place the disk on a resting stand and adjust the drop length of the warps **[N]**.

Finishing

After the beaded braid is your desired length (in this case, 16"), braid another ½" without any beads. Remove any leftover beads from the warps and remove the bobbins. Hold the point of braiding firmly under the disk and remove each warp from

its slot. Tie all eight warps together using an overhand knot. Bind the braid at each end as close as possible to the beads. If you have a focal bead, add it now. Cut off the nubbin very close to the binding **[O]**. For an endcap finish, glue an endcap to each end of the braid **[P]**. Let the glue dry overnight and attach the clasp. For a cone finish, follow the directions on p. 39 for wire-wrapping the cones and assembly.

There doesn't seem to be any place for my beads to go. Is the point of braiding centered in the hole? If not, there won't be enough space between the point of braiding and the foam disk. Tug gently on the warps to move the point of braiding back to center. Try to keep your tension even as you braid so the point of braiding stays centered.

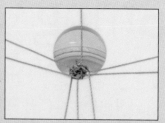

Still no room? Double check that you haven't already moved the cords in this position. Observe which two warps are on top. These two just moved. Their turn is over. If these warps are in the vertical position, you need to turn the disk.

I'm out of beads, but my braid isn't long enough. No problem. Since we measured the beads rather than counting them, it's likely that each warp has a different number of beads. If some of the warps need more beads, just unwind the bobbin, cut off or untie the knot, and use a Big Eye needle to string more beads.

I'm missing a bead! Stay calm. Take a look at your braid. Is the missing bead stuck inside the braid? If so, you may be able to massage it into position. If it's truly missing, you have two options: Continue without it and sew a bead in place when you are finished or braid backward (unbraid) until you come to the mistake and fix it. Remember to fish the beads back out of the braid if you decide to unbraid.

My beads were locking just fine at the beginning of the necklace, but now they keep popping out. Make sure your necklace and the centerweight aren't resting on anything (the table or your lap, for example) while you braid. If the weight isn't dangling, it isn't helping. In fact, if your braid is resting on the table, it may be pushing up above the disk's surface, disrupting the tension you're trying to maintain and leading to "escapee" beads.

What's this bead doing in the middle of my braid? This bead either didn't get placed correctly or it popped out during subsequent moves. Unbraid until you get back to the misplaced bead and reposition it.

See the amber bead in the center?

I'm getting to the end of my beads and the bobbins keep falling off. Ugh. I hate when that happens! Having extra string helps, which is why we used the 3-to-1 rule even though that's a bit excessive for a beaded braid.

Here's my advice: Take some craft scissors (not your good braid-cutting scissors, please!) and make a small cut on the edge of the bobbin. Now you can catch your knot on that and it keeps the bobbin from falling off. Neat trick, eh?

String Theory

I hope you've made a few dozen beaded ropes by now. You've experimented with different color patterns and focal beads. You've probably tried different sizes of seed beads. How'd that go?

No problems with the 11º seed beads. They wouldn't fit on the nylon string, so you used pearl cotton or micro nylon string instead. What about the 6ºs? Everything seemed fine when you were braiding, but now that it's finished, it just doesn't seem right. The braid is squashy—easily compressed and prone to flattening out. Don't worry! We can fix this! Well, not the one you've already done. We'll have to call that a design feature and move on, but we can prevent squashiness in future braids by taking a closer look at string theory.

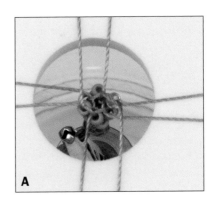

A

We've gotten the hang of locking beads into place while we braid, but what are we really doing to our braid with this process? When we braid with beads, we're arranging the beads in a ring **[A]**. The stringing material is pushed to the center of the ring when we lock a bead in place. That's why you can see the string on the outside of the braid when you forget to lock a bead or if it escapes.

When you use 6º seed beads to make a beaded rope, the large beads formed a large ring, but the stringing material (size 18 nylon string) wasn't thick enough to support the beads. That's why the braid is squashy **[B, C]**.

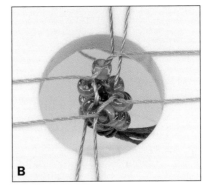

B

There are several strategies for preventing squashiness and creating the firm, round braids you desire:
· Fill the bead hole by using thicker string or multiple strands
· Braid around a core
· Use a combination of bead sizes

The other component to string theory is choosing the right stringing material for your project based on the beads you'll be using. There are several factors to consider when choosing a stringing material:
· Will the string fit easily through the bead hole? (By "easily," I mean can you use a Big Eye needle without having to wrestle the beads?)
· Does the string fill the bead hole?
· How stiff is the string?

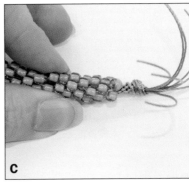

C

In each project in this section, we'll explore one of the squashiness-prevention strategies and discuss the string selection process.

Jumbo Beaded-Rope Bangle

The design challenge: Make a thicker version of the beaded rope by using 6º seed beads, but maintain the firm, round texture of the original size.

Solution: Because 6º seed beads have big holes, the easiest way to prevent squashiness is to double up on stringing material, using two pieces of string per warp.

Finished length: 9" (including clasp; fits 7½" wrist)

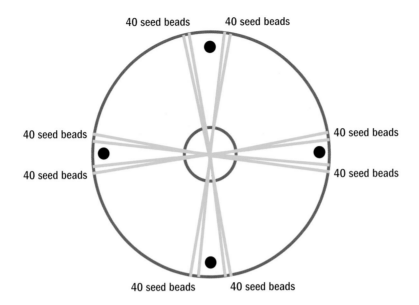

40 seed beads   40 seed beads

40 seed beads

40 seed beads

40 seed beads

40 seed beads

40 seed beads   40 seed beads

YOU'LL NEED

- Beaded Kumihimo Toolkit (use lightest centerweight)

- 12 yd. size 18 nylon string

- 20–25 grams 6º seed beads

- 10mm magnetic endcap

  TIP The nylon string is very firm, and two thicknesses create enough bulk to support the large seed beads. It's easy enough to string the beads by hand, but you can still use a Big Eye needle or bead spinner: Treat the two strings as one as you pass them through the eye of the needle or the thread loop.

Setup

Cut 16 27" pieces of nylon string. Tie them together using an overhand knot. Use two strings per warp and lock them in place on the kumihimo disk in the standard starting position. To keep everything from tangling, wind each warp or pair of strings onto a weighted bobbin.

Take the bobbin off one warp. String 40 6º seed beads on both strings. Tie a knot to keep the beads from falling off. Push the beads together as a group toward the disk so that they are about 2" below it. Starting at the loose end, wind the beaded string onto the bobbin. Keep the beads together as a group so that they don't get tangled with the string. Do this for each of the eight warps.

Braiding

Clip the centerweight below the knot. Braid a ½" nubbin without any beads. Begin adding beads by pushing one bead into the center every time you move a cord. Lock each bead in place by catching it under the cross-warp **[A]**.

Finishing

After you reach your desired length, braid a ½" nubbin without beads. Remove all of the bobbins and the centerweight. Remove the braid from the disk and tie the warps together using an overhand knot. Bind the braid very close to the beads. Cut off both nubbins and glue a magnetic endcap onto each end of the braid.

A

Classic Elegance

I may be biased, but this necklace seems to complement every outfit I wear. It pairs just as well with jeans and a T-shirt as it does with a nice dress. I like the contrast in textures between the faceted fire-polished beads and smooth seed beads.

Finished length: 19" (including clasp)

55

YOU'LL NEED

- Beaded Kumihimo Toolkit
- 6 yd. size 18 nylon string
- 6 yd. size 8 pearl cotton
- 400 4mm fire-polished beads
- 12 grams 8º Japanese seed beads
- 10mm magnetic endcaps

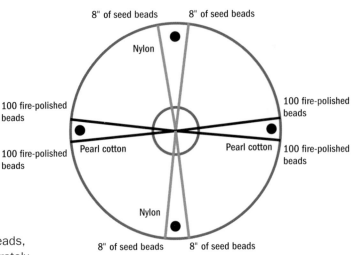

Because we're using two different sizes of beads, consider the stringing material for each separately. The choice of stringing material for the 8º seed beads is easy: We know from experience that size 18 nylon string is a great match. We could also use the nylon string for the fire-polished beads, but their smaller hole size would make that a time-consuming choice. I suggest using thinner and softer size 8 pearl cotton to make stringing easier. Even though we're stringing our large beads on a relatively thin, soft string, the spiraling pattern of smaller seed beads on thicker, stiffer string will support the braid and keep the necklace firm.

Setup

Cut four 1½-yd. pieces of nylon and four 1½-yd. pieces of pearl cotton. Tie them together using an overhand knot and lock them in place on the kumihimo disk in the standard starting position for an eight-warp round braid—nylon in the North and South positions and pearl cotton in the East and West positions. To keep everything from tangling, wind each cord onto a weighted bobbin.

Use a bead spinner to string 8" of 8º seed beads on each warp in the North and South positions. Tie a small knot at the end of the string and then wind the string and beads onto a weighted bobbin.

On each warp in the East and West positions, string 100 fire-polished beads. Fire-polished beads are generally sold temporarily strung. The easiest way to transfer them to the warp is to thread a Big Eye needle on the loose end of pearl cotton. Leaving the fire-polished beads on the cord they came on, start sewing up the strand a few beads at a time. When you have sewn through the entire strand, cut the original cord and remove it **[A]**.

Depending on how many beads are on each strand, you may need to repeat this one or more times for each warp. Tie a small knot at the end of the string and then wind the string and beads onto a weighted bobbin.

Braiding

Clip the centerweight below the knot. Braid a ½" nubbin without any beads. Begin adding beads by pushing one bead into the center every time you move a cord. Lock each bead in place by catching it under the first cord it comes to. It doesn't matter whether you start with the seed beads or the fire-polished beads—just use whatever's easier.

Because of the size difference between the two types of beads, they won't sit as neatly as you're used to **[B]**.

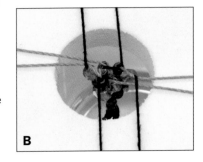

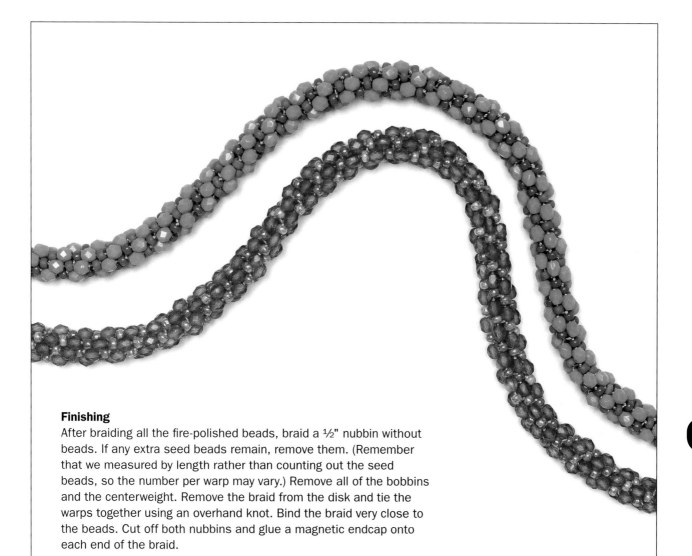

Finishing

After braiding all the fire-polished beads, braid a ½" nubbin without beads. If any extra seed beads remain, remove them. (Remember that we measured by length rather than counting out the seed beads, so the number per warp may vary.) Remove all of the bobbins and the centerweight. Remove the braid from the disk and tie the warps together using an overhand knot. Bind the braid very close to the beads. Cut off both nubbins and glue a magnetic endcap onto each end of the braid.

KUMIHIMO MATH

The bead counts listed yield a necklace approximately 19" long. How many beads should you string if you want a different length?

Because we're using two different sizes of beads, we can't use the seed bead rule of "half the finished length in beads per warp," but we do have enough information to extrapolate how many beads per warp are needed for each inch of braid.

Each warp is strung with 100 beads. The total beaded braid length is 19". 100 divided by 19 is 5.26. That means that this pattern requires 5.26 beads per warp for each inch of finished braid. For example, if you wanted a 22" necklace you would string 116 beads on each warp.

Wait a minute! We're using two different sizes of beads. Why do we use the same number of each type of bead? One bead is added every time a warp is moved and all warps are moved equally, so the same number of beads is used on every warp regardless of bead type or size.

TECHNIQUE: USING DIFFERENT SIZES OF BEADS

Woodland Afternoon

I'm intrigued by the concept of the focal clasp: Bring the hidden into the spotlight. Make the utilitarian beautiful. I like to wear the vintage brass toggle near the front, off to the side near my collarbone. I chose the 11º seed beads for their color, but I was pleased with the way they retreat into the background of the braid. Because of the smaller seed beads, we're using pearl cotton for all eight warps and not just for the fire-polished beads as in the last project. The difference in bead sizes creates a tight spiral and supports the shape of the braid.

Finished length: 21" (including clasp)

YOU'LL NEED
- Beaded Kumihimo Toolkit (use lightest centerweight)
- 12 yd. size 8 pearl cotton
- 400 4mm fire-polished beads
- 10–12 grams 11º Japanese seed beads
- 2 flower endcaps
- 2 2" headpins
- Focal toggle clasp
- 3 16-gauge 5mm ID jump rings
- 6" 26-gauge colored craft wire

8" of seed beads   **8" of seed beads**

100 fire-polished beads (left upper)   **100 fire-polished beads** (right upper)

100 fire-polished beads (left lower)   **100 fire-polished beads** (right lower)

8" of seed beads   **8" of seed beads**

Setup
Cut eight 1½-yd. pieces of pearl cotton. Tie them together using an overhand knot and lock them in place on the kumihimo disk in the standard starting position for an eight-warp round braid. To keep everything from tangling, wind each cord onto a weighted bobbin. Use a bead spinner to string 8" of 11º seed beads on to each warp in the North and South positions. Tie a small knot at the end of the string and then wind the string and beads onto a weighted bobbin. On each warp in the East and West positions, string 100 fire-polished beads. Tie a small knot at the end of the string and then wind the string and beads onto a weighted bobbin.

Braiding
Clip the centerweight below the knot. Braid a ½" nubbin without any beads. Begin adding beads by pushing one bead into the center each time you move a cord. Lock the bead in place by catching the bead under the cross-warp.

Finishing
After braiding all of the fire-polished beads, braid ½" without beads. If there are any extra seed beads, remove them. Remove all of the bobbins and the centerweight. Remove the braid from the disk and tie the warps together using an overhand knot. Bind the braid very close to the beads.

Put an 8º seed bead and a vintage brass flower cap on a headpin. Add another 8º seed bead to the headpin. Make a wire-wrapped loop. Repeat this assembly for the other cap. My falling leaf toggle ring had a hole punched in one end, so I attached it to one of the caps with a jump ring. I wire-wrapped the toggle bar twig: Close one jump ring and hold it centered on the flat side of the twig. Center the craft wire through the ring and using one end of the wire at a time, wrap the wire around the twig and through the jump ring **[A]**. Continue wrapping each end tidily until the wrapped section is about ¼" wide. Make one more wrap with each end of the wire, but this time, wrap only around the jump ring, not the twig **[B]**. Trim the wires close. Attach the twig to the other flower cap using a chain of two jump rings **[C]**. Cut the nubbins off the braid and glue a flower cap over each end. Allow to dry overnight.

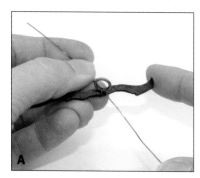

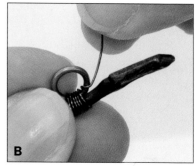

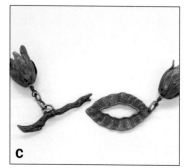

**TECHNIQUE: BRAIDING AROUND A CORE
WITH SMALL-HOLE BEADS**

Fire-Polished Bangle

Braiding with these small-hole 4mm fire-polished beads presents a challenge.
The size 18 nylon string is out because we'd have to string the beads without
a needle and two pieces would not fit through the tiny holes. We'll have to
use pearl cotton, but to prevent squashiness, we'll braid around a satin core.
The core will be wound around a bobbin, but it doesn't get a slot in the disk;
we'll just keep moving it out of the way as we braid.

Finished length: 8" (including magnetic endcaps; fits 6" wrist)

YOU'LL NEED

- Beaded Kumihimo Toolkit
- Extra bobbin (weighted or not)
- 8 yd. size 8 pearl cotton
- 2 ft. 3mm satin cord
- 240 4mm Czech fire-polished beads
- 10mm magnetic endcap set

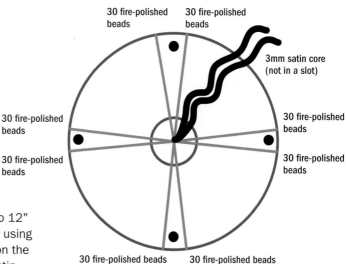

Setup

Cut eight 1-yd. pieces of pearl cotton and two 12" pieces of 3mm satin cord. Tie them together using an overhand knot and lock the pearl cotton on the disk in the standard starting position. The satin doesn't get a slot: Just wind both pieces together on a bobbin and let them hang out anywhere for now. On each of the eight pieces of pearl cotton, string 30 fire-polished beads. Tie a knot at the end of each warp and wind onto a bobbin.

Braiding

As always, begin by attaching the centerweight and braiding a ½" nubbin. What's different this time is that we have to braid around the satin. Just keep moving the satin out of the way as you braid. I like to keep the satin in the Northwest quadrant while I do the "top-right down" move. Then I scoot the satin over to the Northeast quadrant while I do the "bottom-left up" move **[A]**.

After you have a ½" nubbin without beads, start braiding with beads by pushing one bead into the braid every time you move a warp. Be sure to catch the bead under the first cross-warp it comes to. Move the satin core out of the way as you work **[B]**.

KUMIHIMO MATH

30 beads per warp yields an 8" bracelet. 30 divided by 8 is 3.75. Let's round that up to four and say that for every inch of braid you need four fire-polished beads per warp. That means if you want this project to be 9" long, you'd string 36 beads per warp.

After you have braided all of the beads, braid a ½" nubbin without beads. Remove the braid from the disk and tie an overhand knot.

Finishing

Bind the braid near the beads and cut off the excess braid. Glue on endcaps and allow to dry.

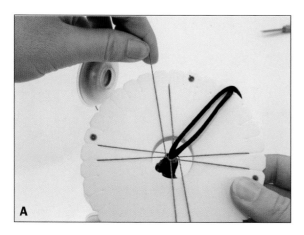

A

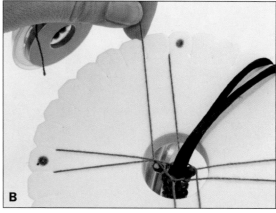

B

Jasper Canyon

This necklace is another variation on creating a textural spiral with different sizes of beads (in this case, bird's eye rhyolite gemstones, fire-polished beads, and seed beads). The spiral is in the front of the necklace and thread will show, so consider that as you select your stringing material.

Finished length: 18"

YOU'LL NEED

- Beaded kumihimo tool kit

- White glue

- 12 yd. size 18 nylon string

- 16 grams 8º Japanese seed beads

- 150 4mm round gemstone beads

- 50 4mm fire-polished beads

- 8mm endcap set with integral hook-and-eye clasp

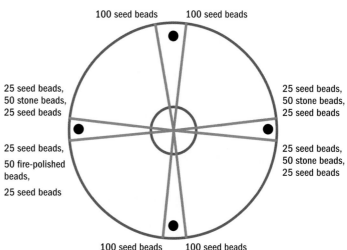

The choice for the four warps carrying 8º seed beads is obvious: size 18 nylon string. This pairing works brilliantly. The other four warps will carry two types of beads: either gemstones and seed beads or fire-polished beads and seed beads. We could use pearl cotton for these four warps because it fits easily through the holes of both the stones and fire-polished; however, because of the seed-bead-only sections at the beginning and end of the braid, we need nylon string for all the warps to keep those sections smooth. The nylon does not fit easily through either the fire-polished or stone beads when you use a needle, but if you stiffen the end with glue and work without a needle, you can string those beads easily.

Setup

Cut eight 1½-yd. pieces of nylon. Tie them together using an overhand knot and lock them in place on the disk in the standard starting position for an eight-warp round braid. To keep everything from tangling, wind each cord onto a weighted bobbin.

String 100 8º seed beads on each warp in the North and South positions. Tie a small knot at the end of the string and then wind the string and beads onto a weighted bobbin.

On both warps in the East position and one warp in the West position, string beads in the following pattern: 25 8º seed beads, 50 4mm gemstone beads, 25 seed beads. Tie a small knot at the end of the string and wind the string and beads onto a weighted bobbin.

On the remaining warp in the West position, string beads in the following pattern: 25 seed beads, 50 4mm fire-polished beads, 25 seed beads. Tie a small knot at the end of the string and wind the string and beads onto a weighted bobbin.

Braiding

Clip the centerweight below the knot. Braid a ½" nubbin without any beads. Begin adding beads by pushing one bead to the center every time you move a cord. Lock the bead in place by catching it under the first cord it meets.

Finishing

After braiding all the beads, braid a ½" section without beads. Remove all the bobbins and the centerweight. Remove the braid from the disk and tie the warps together using an overhand knot. Bind the braid very close to the beads. Cut off both nubbins and glue an endcap onto each end of the braid.

Braiding with Teardrops

Teardrops are a fun shape to braid with. My favorites are handmade borosilicate glass teardrop beads: full, plump teardrops with large holes.

The plump teardrops I'm especially fond of are made by Unicorne Beads. Several styles of Czech teardrop and dagger beads are available too. They are thinner and have much smaller holes.

Braiding with teardrops is much like braiding with any other bead—just lock a bead in place when you move a warp. Be sure that it's the hole-end of the bead that catches. You want the fuller end of the teardrop to point away from the center of the

braid **[A]**. For the most part, the beads will do this automatically, but you still want to keep an eye on them. The boro glass teardrops are heavy—so heavy that we won't string them until we're ready to use them so their weight doesn't mess with the tension.

A

Boro glass teardrops work beautifully in kumihimo. The regular size is 7x9mm; mini teardrops are 5x7mm.

Czech drops and daggers are slender with small holes.

Polka Dot Daisies

A pattern can define a necklace's personality. To me the polka-dot daisy pattern says "fun and playful." Remember that the color pattern is determined by the placement of the warps as you set up the braid.

Finished length: 18½" (including clasp)

YOU'LL NEED

- Beaded Kumihimo Tool Kit

- 12 yd. size 18 nylon string (9 yd. white, 3 yd. black)

- 24 grams 8⁰ Japanese seed beads (18 grams white, 6 grams black)

- 50 7x9mm black Unicorne teardrop beads (regular size)

- 2 8mm black enameled flower caps

- 1 black-and-white enameled hook-and-eye clasp

- 2 2" copper headpins

- 6 4mm ID copper jump rings

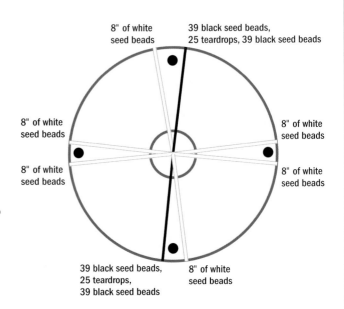

Setup

Cut eight 54" warps (six white and two black). Tie them together using an overhand knot and lock each warp in place in the standard starting position: one black warp in the right-side North position and the other black warp in the left-side South position.

On each of the white warps, string 8" of white 8⁰ seed beads. Tie a small knot at the end of each warp so the beads don't fall off. Wrap each warp onto a bobbin. On each of the two black warps, string 39 black 8⁰ seed beads. These two black warps will eventually carry the teardrop beads as well, but we're leaving them off for now so the heavy teardrops don't cause uneven tension in the first part of the braid.

Braiding

Attach the centerweight and braid ½" without any beads. Begin adding beads by pushing one bead into the center each time you move a cord. Lock the bead in place by catching the bead under the cross-warp. Continue until you have used all of the black seed beads previously strung.

Braiding with teardrops

On each of the black warps, string 25 teardrops and 39 seed beads. Wind the string and seed beads onto the bobbin, but don't try to fit the teardrops into the bobbin. Just let them hang between the bottom of the disk and the top of the bobbin. Resume braiding. The teardrops are added in the same way as the seed beads. The only

special consideration is to be sure the narrow part of the teardrop is locked under the cross-cord and the rounded part of the teardrop points away from the point of braiding.

Finishing

After braiding all of the black beads, braid a ½" section without beads. Remove all of the bobbins, any leftover white seed beads, and the centerweight. Remove the braid from the disk and tie the warps together using an overhand knot.

Bind the braid very close to the beads.

Put a flower cap on the headpin so that the head is inside the cone and the pin is sticking out of the top. String a seed bead. Make a wire-wrapped loop. Repeat this assembly for the other cone. Use jump rings to attach the clasp.

Cut the braid at either end very close to the binding. Glue on the flower caps using E6000.

TECHNIQUE: BRAIDING WITH MINI TEARDROPS

Amber Sunset

These mini teardrops are perfect for scaling down to bracelet size. You'll pair 11º seed beads with the mini teardrops.

Finished length: 7" (fits 6" wrist)

YOU'LL NEED

- Beaded Kumihimo Toolkit
- 8 yd. size 8 pearl cotton
- 50 5x7mm Unicorne teardrops (mini size)
- 5 grams 11º Japanese seed beads
- 2 6mm cones
- Toggle clasp
- 2 2" headpins
- 2 4x6mm jump rings
- E6000 glue

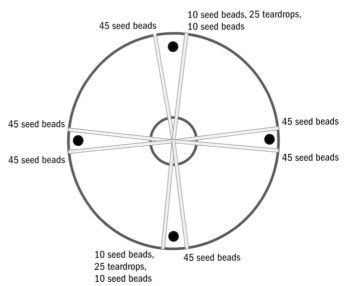

45 seed beads

10 seed beads, 25 teardrops, 10 seed beads

45 seed beads

45 seed beads

45 seed beads

45 seed beads

45 seed beads

10 seed beads, 25 teardrops, 10 seed beads

45 seed beads

Setup
Cut eight 24" warps and tie them together using an overhand knot. Lock each warp in place on the disk in the standard starting position.

On the East and West warps as well as the left-side North warp and right-side South warp (that's six warps total), string 45 11º seed beads. Tie a small knot at the end of each warp. Starting with the end with the knot, wind the pearl cotton onto the bobbin, winding most of the pearl cotton first and then the beads as a group. Close the bobbin over the beads.

On the remaining two warps (right-side North and left-side South), string the following pattern: 10 11º seed beads, 25 mini teardrops, 10 seed beads. Tie a small knot at the end of each warp. Starting with the end with the knot, wind the pearl cotton onto the bobbin with the majority of the pearl cotton first, then the beads as a group. Close the bobbin over as many beads as will comfortably fit.

> **TIP We normally wait to string the teardrops until just before we use them, but for this bracelet, the seed-bead-only section is so short that it doesn't matter.**

Braiding
Attach the centerweight and braid ½" without any beads. Begin adding beads by pushing one bead into the center each time you move a cord. Lock the bead in place by catching the bead on the first cord it meets. Because the 11º's are so small, it's extra important that you use a gentle touch and give the pearl cotton plenty of slack as you position the first few beads [A].

Finishing
After braiding all of the beads, braid a ½" section without beads. Remove all of the bobbins and the centerweight. Tie the warps together using an overhand knot.

Bind the braid very close to the beads.

Put the cone on the headpin so the head is inside the cone and the pin extends out of the top. Make a wire-wrapped loop. Repeat this assembly for the other cone. Use jump rings to attach the toggle bar to one cone and the toggle ring to the other cone.

Cut the braid at either end very close to the binding. Glue on the cones using E6000.

A

My bracelet is 7" long and fits a 6" wrist. The teardrop center section is 3" long. On each side is 1" of beaded braid with 11º seed beads. The cones and toggle clasp add about 2".

The easiest place to add length is in the seed bead sections. For every inch of finished braid you'd like to add, you'll need 10 additional seed beads per warp. It's best to make this bracelet snug so the mini teardrops don't roll to the bottom of your wrist.

Amber Sunset bracelet length options

Finished length	Setup for warps A & B	Setup for all other warps
7"	10 11º seed beads, 25 mini teardrops, 10 seed beads	45 seed beads
8"	15 seed beads, 25 mini teardrops, 15 seed beads	55 seed beads
9"	20 seed beads, 25 mini teardrops, 20 seed beads	65 seed beads

Cone and toggle 1"

Seed beads 1"

Mini teardrop center section 3"

Seed beads 1"

Cone and toggle 1"

69

The Showstopper

This is one of my "going out" necklaces. Be prepared to be stopped by strangers on the street asking where you got your fabulous necklace. Smile big when you tell them you made it yourself!

Finished length: 17½" (including endcaps)

YOU'LL NEED

- Beaded Kumihimo Toolkit
- 12 yd. size 18 nylon string
- 25 grams 8° Japanese seed beads
- 8 grams 6° Japanese seed beads
- 50 7x9mm Unicorne teardrop beads (regular size)
- 50 5x7 Unicorne teardrop beads (mini size)
- 8mm magnetic endcap

Setup

Cut eight 54" warps and tie them together using an overhand knot. Lock each warp in place in the standard starting position.

On every warp except the top-right position and the bottom-left position, string 99 8° seed beads (that's about 8" if you'd rather measure than count). Tie a small knot at the end of each warp so the beads don't fall off. Wrap each warp onto a bobbin. Mark the top-right bobbin A and the bottom-left bobbin B. (I mark the washer with a Sharpie and erase it later with rubbing alcohol.) Warps A and B will carry both seed beads and teardrops, but to keep the weight balanced for now, string this pattern on each: 15 8° seed beads and 10 6° seed beads. Wind each warp onto a bobbin.

Braiding

Attach the centerweight and braid a ½" nubbin without beads. The next time it's warp A's turn to move, begin braiding with beads. Lock each bead in place by catching it against the first cross-warp it meets. When you are out of beads on warps A and B, it's time to string more beads. String both warp A and warp B with the following pattern: 12 mini teardrops, 25 teardrops, 12 mini teardrops, 10 6° seed beads, and 15 8° seed beads.

Wind each warp back onto its bobbin and continue braiding as usual, adding one bead to the braid in every move. When you are out of beads on warps A and B (you may have leftover beads on the other warps if you measured rather than counted), braid a ½" nubbin without beads. Remove the braid from the disk and tie with an overhand knot. Bind close to the beads. Trim the braid and glue on endcaps as usual.

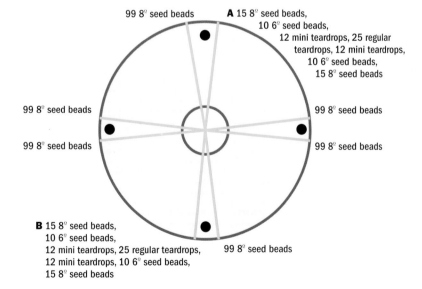

Using Long Magatama Beads

Long magatama beads are a seed bead shape that is sort of a cross between flower petals and daggers. They are made by the Japanese seed bead manufacturer Miyuki.

These asymmetrical beads are fun and challenging to work with. They have a front and a back as well as a top and bottom, so you have to decide up front whether you're going to take the time to string them all facing the same direction or let them face every which way. Both approaches result in interesting textures. For the Dragonscale necklace, the magatama face the same direction, creating an elegant scale texture. In the Magatama Spiral, the randomness of the beads gives the piece a botanical feel.

Let's take a closer look at the magatama beads. Pour some out on the fuzzy beading mat. The trick to lining these up in one direction is to pay attention to the hole. The hole is angled. I'm right-handed, so when I string beads with the needle in my right hand, I'm working from right to left. For me it's easiest if the hole is pointing down and to the left **[A, left two columns]**. In this orientation the hole is on the right side of the bead at the very far edge. The hole slopes downward toward the middle of the bead.

If you flip the bead over, you'll notice that the hole is situated closer to the middle of the bead **[A, right column]**. In this orientation the hole is sloping down to the right. Laying out the beads in this position is often more comfortable for left-handed people.

If a project calls for the magatama to be strung in the same direction, they can be strung either way shown here, as long as they all face the same direction.

Let's practice first. With the unthreaded needle, pick up five magatama. Hold the needle horizontally. Do all the beads point in the same direction? Yes **[B]**. Very good! Now hold the needle vertically. Can you still tell if they magatama are pointing the same direction? Maybe, but it's harder because they start flipping around **[C]**. Now you know that it's best to check your beads when they are hanging horizontally.

The braiding action using magatama is not much different from braiding with seed beads or fire-polished beads. Every time you move a cord, you'll slide a bead into the center of the braid and catch it under the cross-warp. Pay attention to the long end and the short end: You want to catch the short end (the end with the hole) under the thread so that the long end points to the outside of the braid. For the most part, the magatama will naturally fall into the correct position, but sometimes they flip around and try to catch on the long side. After the first few rounds, you'll find your rhythm and they'll go into place more easily, but you must remain vigilant for the entire length of the braid.

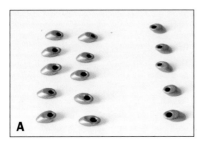

A

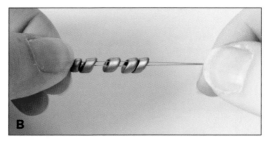

B

C

Dragonscale

I have always enjoyed fantasy novels about dragons. Dragons are exciting and dangerous, but also beautiful and majestic. When I first spotted this toggle clasp, I knew I had to make a special necklace for it. Upon closer inspection, the clasp is actually a snake for the ring and a lizard for the bar, but I always see a dragon.

For this project, it's very important that all of the magatama beads face the same direction when strung to achieve the smooth, elegant scale texture.

Finished length: 18" (including clasp)

YOU'LL NEED

- Beaded Kumihimo Toolkit

- About 70 grams Miyuki long (4x7mm) magatama beads (50 grams color A/green, 20 grams color B/bronze)

- 5 grams 8º Japanese seed beads

- 12 yd. size 18 twisted nylon cord

- 2 8mm bronze cones

- Focal toggle clasp

- 2 2" copper or bronze headpins

- 4 4x6mm oval jump rings

- E6000 glue

5 seed beads,
69 green magatama,
5 seed beads

5 seed beads,
69 bronze magatama,
5 seed beads

5 seed beads,
69 green magatama,
5 seed beads

5 seed beads,
69 green magatama,
5 seed beads

5 seed beads,
69 green magatama,
5 seed beads

5 seed beads,
69 green magatama,
5 seed beads

5 seed beads,
69 bronze magatama,
5 seed beads

5 seed beads,
69 green magatama,
5 seed beads

Setup

Cut eight 54" warps, tie them together using an overhand knot, and lock them in place in the standard starting position. On each warp, string the following pattern: 5 8º seed beads, 69 magatama (all facing the same direction), 5 seed beads. Tie a small knot at the end of each warp so the beads don't fall off. Wrap each warp onto a bobbin.

In addition to checking that all magatama on a warp face the same direction, it's very important to check that all warps have matching magatama orientation: Double-check that all the magatama either point toward the disk or toward the bobbins. It won't work if the magatama on some warps point toward the disk and the magatama on other warps point toward the bobbin.

Braiding

Braid ½" without any beads. This will serve as a place for binding when finished.

Begin adding beads by pushing one bead into the center each time you move a cord.

Finishing

After braiding all of the beads, braid a ½" section without beads. Remove all of the bobbins and the centerweight. Remove the braid from the disk and tie the warps together using an overhand knot.

Bind the braid very close to the beads.

Place a seed bead, a bronze cone, and a seed bead on a headpin. Make a wire-wrapped loop. Repeat this assembly for the other cone. Use jump rings to attach the toggle bar to one cone and the toggle ring to the other cone.

Cut each end of the braid very close to the binding. Glue on the cones using E6000.

These magatama all point toward the bobbin.

**TECHNIQUE: USING RANDOMLY STRUNG
LONG MAGATAMA BEADS**

Magatama Spiral

For this project, we'll string the magatama beads facing every which way to get a random, organic texture. We're also incorporating round seed beads to space out the magatama in the braid, allowing us to better appreciate their unusual shape. The spiral pattern is soothing and helps to calm the chaos a bit.

Finished length: 8½" (fits 7" wrist)

YOU'LL NEED

- Beaded Kumihimo Toolkit
- 8 yd. size 18 twisted nylon cord
- 17 grams 4x7mm Miyuki long magatama beads
- 10 grams 8º Japanese seed beads
- 2 flower cones
- Toggle clasp
- 2 2" headpins
- 2 4x6mm oval jump rings

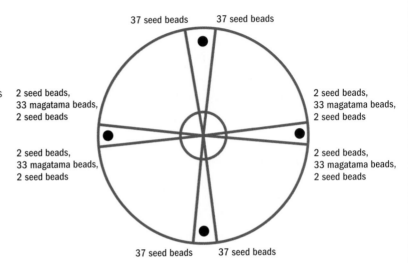

37 seed beads   37 seed beads

2 seed beads,
33 magatama beads,
2 seed beads

2 seed beads,
33 magatama beads,
2 seed beads

2 seed beads,
33 magatama beads,
2 seed beads

2 seed beads,
33 magatama beads,
2 seed beads

37 seed beads   37 seed beads

Setup

Cut eight 24" warps, tie them together using an overhand knot, and lock them in place in the standard starting position. On each of the warps in the North and South positions, string 37 8º seed beads. On each warp in the East and West positions, string the following pattern: 2 8º seed beads, 33 magatama beads, 2 8º seed beads. For this project, it doesn't matter which direction the magatama beads face; string the points every which way.

Tie a small knot at the end of each warp so the beads don't fall off. Wind each warp onto a bobbin.

Braiding

Attach the centerweight and braid a ½" nubbin without any beads. Begin adding beads by pushing one bead into the center each time you move a cord. Lock the bead in place by catching the bead under the first cord it meets. Make sure that the long ends of the magatama beads point away from the braid.

Finishing

After braiding all of the beads, braid a ½" section without beads. Remove all the bobbins and the centerweight. Tie the warps together using an overhand knot.

Bind the braid very close to the beads.

Place a seed bead, a flower cone, and another seed bead on a headpin. Make a wire-wrapped loop. Repeat this assembly for the other cone.

Use a headpin to make a wrapped loop on the toggle bar. Use jump rings to attach the toggle bar to one cone and the toggle ring to the other cone.

Cut the braid ends very close to the binding. Secure the braids in the cones with glue.

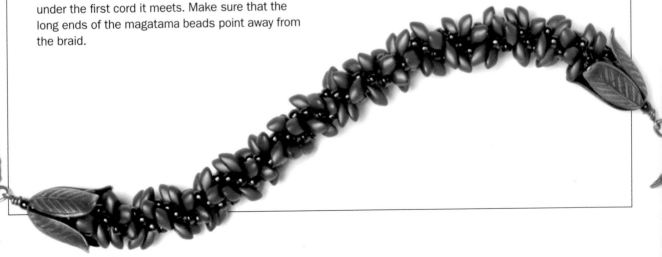

Counted Patterns

Now that you're an experienced braider, it's time to become more familiar with the structure of the braid. Although I show photos, what I'm about to explain will make more sense if you have a 3-D model in your hand. I'll wait right here while you make it. It won't take long.

YOU'LL NEED
- Beaded Kumihimo Toolkit
- 8 ft. size 18 nylon string
- 120 black 8º Japanese seed beads
- 20 white 8º Japanese seed beads
- 5 8º Japanese seed beads in each of 4 colors: red, blue, green, and yellow

A note about the colors: We're not making a fashion statement here. We want opaque, plain-finish beads that are easy to see. You'll defeat the purpose if you make the model using six shades of purple.

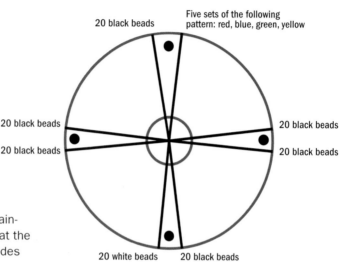

20 black beads

Five sets of the following pattern: red, blue, green, yellow

20 black beads

20 black beads

20 black beads

20 black beads

20 white beads   20 black beads

Setup
Cut eight 12" warps, tie them together using an overhand knot, and lock them in place on the disk in the standard starting position. On the top-right warp, string five sets of the following pattern: red, blue, green, yellow. Tie a knot at the end and wind the warp onto a bobbin. On the bottom-left warp, string 20 white beads. Tie a knot at the end and wind onto a bobbin. On each of the remaining six warps, string 20 black beads, tie a knot at the end, and wind onto a bobbin.

Braiding
Attach the centerweight and braid a ½" nubbin without beads. Begin braiding with beads, making sure that the first bead added is a red one. Keep braiding with beads until you have used all of the beads. Braid a ½" nubbin without beads. Remove the braid from the disk and tie an overhand knot.

See, that didn't take long at all. Welcome back! Now let's take a look at your 3-D model.

We used the basic round braid moves: top-right down and bottom-left up. Although these moves are done one at a time (because most of us only have two hands), think of them as occurring in unison. Each movement—either top-right down or bottom-left up—is half of a set. Think of warps that move together in this way as dance partners: One steps forward and the other steps back, but they always move together. There are four sets of partners in every eight-warp round braid. In our model, the warp with colored beads and the warp with white beads are partners. All of the other partner sets have black beads. This color contrast will help us follow the movement of the beads around the braid.

Holding the braid vertically with the starting knot pointing up, look at the beginning of the braid. Notice that the first beads added were red and white and they are opposite of each other. This is always the case with partner warps.

Observe the path of these two warps: the colored and the white **[A]**. Look for the first blue bead. That's the next bead added from the colored warp. Notice that again there is a white bead from its partner warp directly opposite. Also observe the orientation of this second set of partner beads in relation to the first set of partner beads. The second set is rotated counterclockwise 90 degrees from the first set. This 90-degree rotation continues, positioning the green bead (third in the sequence) 180 degrees from the red bead (first in the sequence) **[B]**. The yellow bead, fourth in the sequence, is 270 degrees from the first red bead **[C]**. One more 90-degree rotation brings us back to the beginning, and the next red bead is in line with all the red beads.

Turn the braid horizontally so the first red bead is on your left **[D]**. Look at that! All the red beads line up neatly in a row. Directly opposite the braid from this neat line of red beads is an equally neat row of partner white beads. Now imagine that all the red beads are some sort of fabulous drop bead. Are

you as excited about this as I am? We just learned two very useful design features of this braid.

First, by stringing the beads as four-bead units, the first beads in the units will all lie on the same side of the braid.

For example: dropbead, regular bead, regular bead, regular bead, dropbead, regular bead, regular bead, regular bead.

The first beads in the units will be spaced about ⅝" apart (when using 8º seed beads).

A

B

C

D

TECHNIQUE: COUNTED PATTERNS

The Countess

This necklace could be made with a variety of drop beads. I used pebble beads and teardrop beads in mine, but it would be fun to try it with daggers or Czech drops as well.

Finished length: 18¾" (including endcaps)

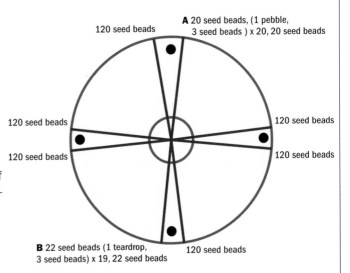

YOU'LL NEED
- Beaded Kumihimo Toolkit
- 12 yd. size 18 nylon string
- 20 grams 8º Japanese seed beads
- 19 7x9mm Unicorne teardrop beads (regular size)
- 20 Unicorne 5x8mm pebble beads (mini size) or 5x7mm teardrop beads (mini size)
- 8mm magnetic endcap

Setup
Cut eight 54" warps, tie them together using an overhand knot, and lock them on the disk in the standard starting position. On each warp except the top-right and bottom-left, string 120 8º seed beads (about 10"). Tie a small knot at the end of each warp and wind onto a bobbin. Mark the top-right bobbin "A" and the bottom-left bobbin "B."

Warps A and B will carry both seed beads and teardrops/pebbles, but to keep the weight balanced for now, string 20 8º seed beads on warp A and 22 8º seed beads on warp B. Wind each onto a bobbin.

This Countess necklace was made with regular-size teardrops alternating with mini pebbles.

A 20 seed beads, (1 pebble, 3 seed beads) x 20, 20 seed beads

120 seed beads

120 seed beads

120 seed beads

120 seed beads

120 seed beads

120 seed beads

B 22 seed beads (1 teardrop, 3 seed beads) x 19, 22 seed beads

120 seed beads

Braiding
Attach the centerweight and braid a ½" nubbin without beads. The next time it's warp A's turn to move, begin braiding with beads. Lock each bead in place by catching it under the first cross-warp it meets. When you are out of beads on warps A and B, it's time to string more beads.

On warp A, string 20 sets of this pattern: pebble bead, 3 seed beads. After that, string 20 seed beads. On warp B, string 19 sets of this pattern: teardrop bead, 3 seed beads. After that, string 22 seed beads. Wind each warp back onto its bobbin and continue braiding as usual, adding one bead to the braid with every move. When you are out of beads on warps A and B (you may have leftover beads on the other warps if you measured rather than counted), braid a ½" nubbin without beads.

Finishing
Remove the braid from the disk and tie an overhand knot. Bind close to the beads. Trim the braid and glue on endcaps as usual.

This version uses regular and mini sizes of boro glass teardrops.

Adding a Pendant

In a necklace such as the Beaded Rope, you can slip a large-hole art glass bead over the braid as a focal point. In the Dragonscale and Woodland Afternoon necklaces, toggle clasps take center stage. As much as I adore art glass and focal clasps, there's a great big world of beads out there. So let's take a peek at pendants.

I'm going to show you four different techniques for adding a pendant or focal bead other than the obvious "pick one big enough to slide on." With these techniques in your repertoire, no focal bead will be off-limits to you.

The first option, as you'll see in the mini project that follows, is to choose endcaps that double as a bail. I know it seems too easy, but it's a great trick and the perfect solution for beads with small holes that won't accommodate the eight warp strings.

In Moonlit Lagoon, we'll attach an artisan glass donut using a lark's head knot. This simple technique just requires a bit of forethought. I'll show you how to measure your donut bead using a test cord to ensure a good fit.

In Five Marbles and Stuck in the Middle, we break one of the cardinal rules learned when we did the Basic Braid. Are you sitting down? We remove all eight warps from the disk midway through the braiding, add a focal bead, and then put the braid back on the disk. Gasp! I know I said never to do this, but you're ready. Here's the secret: Because the beaded braid portions of the necklace sit very snugly next to the focal bead, as long as we're neat and tidy, it doesn't matter whether we get the warps exactly as they were. It's as though we're starting the braid fresh from a knot.

I took the warps off the disk, strung the focal bead, and placed the warps back into position to resume braiding. If some of the warps end up in different positions than before, it's OK.

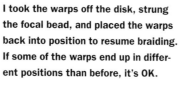

Moonlit Lagoon uses a simple lark's head knot attachment.

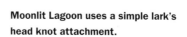

And because I'd be remiss as a teacher if I didn't challenge you, in Beaded Pass-Through, we're going to remove the warps from the disk mid-braid, but this time we'll make sure we put everything back in the correct point of braiding. It matters because a fiber-focused necklace will show any mistakes made putting the warps back in the place. I know this is scary. I'll show you two different techniques: one baby-step method and the other a great big leap. In the baby-steps method, we'll remove each warp in turn and pass it down through the center hole of the disk, pass it through the focal bead, and then return it to the correct position on the disk. Taking the great leap, we'll remove all eight warps at once, add the pendant, and return the warps to the disk. In both techniques, we'll carefully observe the point of braiding to be sure we have the correct over-under interlacement that creates the braid.

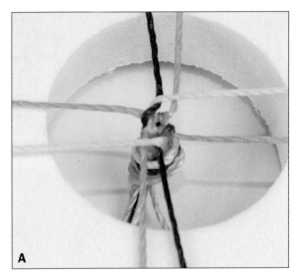

A

Point of braiding

What do I mean by that? Look at this point of braiding **[A]**. (If you have a braid in progress, that's an even better visual aid.) Starting with the left-side North warp and working clockwise, observe the orientation of each warp.

The left-side North warp (brown) starts on the left-side of the point of braiding, crosses over the upper West warp (gold), and passes under the upper East warp (cream). The upper East warp (cream) is pulling the left-side North warp (brown) toward the middle of the braid.

On this turn, the right-side North warp (green) is ready to move. This warp and its partner warp (the other green warp) are the lowest warps in the braid. This warp exits the braid from the top right and passes under the upper East warp (cream).

The upper East warp (cream) exits the braid from the top and crosses over both the North warps. It just moved last turn.

The lower East warp (gold) starts at the top of the point of braiding and passes under the right-side South warp (brown). The right-side South warp (brown) is pulling the lower East warp (gold) down so it exits the point of braid at the lower right.

The right-side South warp (brown) starts on the right side of the point of braiding, crosses over the lower East warp (gold), and passes under the lower West warp (cream). The lower West warp (cream) is pulling the right-side South warp (brown) toward the middle.

The left-side South warp (green) is ready to move this turn. This warp and its partner warp (the other green warp) are the lowest warps in the braid. It exits the braid from the bottom left and passes under the lower West warp (cream).

The lower West warp (cream) exits the braid from the bottom and crosses over both the South warps. It just moved last turn.

The upper West warp (gold) starts at the bottom of the point of braiding and passes under the left-side North warp (brown). The left-side North warp (brown) is pulling the upper West warp (gold) up so it exits the point of braiding at the upper left.

Using endcaps with a built-in bail

YOU'LL NEED

- Beaded Kumihimo Toolkit
- Beaded braid
- Magnetic endcap set with built-in bail
- Focal bead and 2 coordinating accent beads
- Headpin
- Jump ring

This mini project shows you one easy way to add a pendant thanks to an ingenious magnetic endcap set that also functions as a bail: You simply attach a focal bead to it and wear it in front. You can easily swap out the focal bead just by opening and closing the jump ring.

Start with a completed beaded braid (removed from the disk). Arrange the accent beads and focal bead on a headpin. Make a wire-wrapped loop over the beads. Attach the wrapped loop to the endcap loop using a jump ring **[A]**. Bind the braid near the beads. Cut off the excess braid, glue on the endcaps, and allow to dry overnight.

A

Moonlit Lagoon

This project is a variation on the Classic Elegance necklace. Because the cord is visible in the center, I used pearl cotton for all eight warps. It makes a delicate, smooth braid, although the beaded braid portion is a bit on the squashy side.

Finished length: 21" (including endcaps)

YOU'LL NEED

- Beaded Kumihimo Toolkit (use lightest centerweight)
- 12 yd. size 8 pearl cotton
- 400 4mm fire-polished beads
- 12 grams 8° Japanese seed beads
- Artisan glass donut pendant
- 10mm magnetic endcap set

Setup

Cut eight 54" warps, tie them together using an overhand knot, and lock them on the disk in the standard starting position. On each warp in the East and West positions, string 4" of 8° seed beads. Don't tie a knot at the end because we'll add more beads later. Wind each warp onto a bobbin. On each warp in the North and South positions, string 50 4mm fire-polished beads. Don't tie a knot at the end because we'll add more beads later. Wind each warp onto a bobbin.

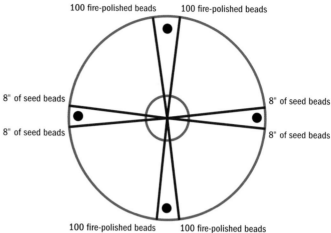

100 fire-polished beads   100 fire-polished beads

8" of seed beads   8" of seed beads

8" of seed beads   8" of seed beads

100 fire-polished beads   100 fire-polished beads

KUMIHIMO MATH

Here's how to determine how long to make the unbeaded center section of your braid based on the dimensions of your donut.

Find a scrap of 1mm satin cord (its diameter is very similar to our unbeaded center section). Make a lark's head knot around the donut **[A]**. With a permanent marker, mark the cords where they exit the knot and then untie the knot **[B]**. The distance between the two marks is the minimum length needed for the unbeaded center section **[C]**.

One more quick test—take the scrap cord that you marked and bring the two marks together to make a loop. Is the loop big enough to fit over the beaded braid? (You can test this even if your braid is still on the disk.) If the answer is yes, so far so good. Otherwise, increase the size of the loop. Mark the increased size and measure, and make the unbeaded center section that length.

A

B

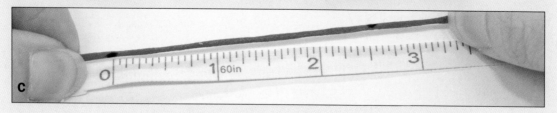

C

A

B

C

D

Braiding

Attach the centerweight and braid a ½" nubbin without beads. Begin braiding with beads by locking one bead in place every time you move a warp. It doesn't matter if you start with the fire-polished or the seed beads. Continue braiding with beads until you are out of fire-polished beads, remove any extra seed beads, and then braid an unbeaded center section. (See "Kumihimo Math" to determine how long this section should be based on your pendant.)

On each warp in the East and West positions, string 4" of 8° seed beads and wind each warp onto a bobbin. On each warp in the North and South positions, string 50 4mm fire-polished beads. Wind each warp onto a bobbin. Continue braiding with beads until you are out of fire-polished beads.

Because we measured the seed beads rather than counted them, you may need to add or remove seed beads. Braid a ½" nubbin without beads. Remove the braid from the disk and tie an overhand knot.

Adding the pendant with a lark's head knot

Fold the braid in half **[A]**. The folded midpoint of the braid should be the center of the unbeaded center section. Bring this fold through the donut's hole **[B]**.

One at a time, bring each end of the braid through the loop formed by the fold **[C]** and tighten the knot **[D]**.

Finishing

Bind each end of the braid very close to the beads. Cut off the excess braid and glue on the endcaps.

Five Marbles

You'll be a pro at adding focal beads to your kumihimo after you add five to this necklace. For the base beaded braid, I used a mix of seed beads and blended them in my bead spinner. I like how the different blues play together.

Finished length: 19" (including endcaps)

YOU'LL NEED

- Beaded Kumihimo Toolkit

- 12 yd. size 18 nylon string

- 5 focal beads of graduated sizes (1 large, 2 medium, 2 small) each with a hole large enough to fit 8 pieces of nylon string

- 20 grams 8º Japanese seed beads

- 2 8mm endcaps

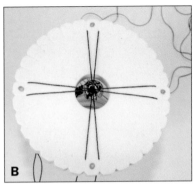

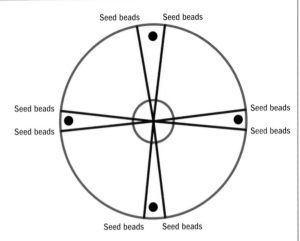

Seed beads · Seed beads
Seed beads · Seed beads
Seed beads · Seed beads
Seed beads · Seed beads

Setup

Cut eight 54" pieces of string, tie them together using an overhand knot, and lock the warps on the disk in the standard starting position. On each warp, string 3" of seed beads (See "Kumihimo Math" to learn how I determined this number). Don't tie a knot at the end of each warp—we'll need to add more beads again soon. Wind each warp onto a weighted bobbin.

Braiding

Attach the centerweight and braid a ½" nubbin without beads. Begin braiding with beads, starting with a "top-right down" move. Lock each bead in place by tucking it under the first cross-warp it meets. When the beaded braid is 6" long, stop adding beads and braid ⅜" (just shy of the width of the smallest focal bead) without beads. Clip the centerweight just below the point of braiding and remove the bobbins and any leftover seed beads. Remove the braid from the disk.

Adding a focal bead

Pull all eight warps through the focal bead **[A]**. Remove the centerweight and position the focal bead snugly against the beaded braid. With the beaded braid and focal bead below the disk, pull the loose warps up through the center hole. Lock the warps back on the disk in the standard starting position. It doesn't matter where they were before; just arrange them in the standard starting position. With the warps neatly exiting the focal bead, pull the warps flush against the face of the disk **[B]**.

More stringing and braiding

String six seed beads on each warp and wind the warps back onto bobbins. Replace the centerweight at the end of the braid. Braid 8–12 moves without adding any beads. (Top-right down is the first move;

bottom-left up is the second. Don't count turning.) This repositions the warps and create the over-under point of braiding necessary to lock the beads into place. This also gives you enough space for the first seed beads. Exactly how many braiding moves to make without beads depends on the shape of your focal bead. Begin braiding with beads, locking a bead in place with each move. If the first few beads refuse to stay in place, try doing a few more moves without beads first.

Continue braiding with beads until you run out of beads. Braid without beads until you have a nubbin slightly shorter than the next focal bead. Repeat "Adding a focal bead" and "More stringing and braiding" until you have added all five focal beads.

After adding the last focal bead, string 3" of seed beads on each warp and braid until you have 6" of beaded braid after the last focal bead. Double check to make sure that the necklace is even. When you are satisfied, braid a ½" nubbin without beads. Remove the braid from the disk and tie an overhand knot. Bind close to the beads. Trim the braid and glue on endcaps as usual.

KUMIHIMO MATH

My set of five focal beads is 2" long and I wanted 1" of beaded braid between each bead; thus my focal section needed to be 6". I subtracted the 6" focal section from my 18" target total length and got 12". Dividing that by two, I knew that I needed 6" of beaded braid on each side of my focal section. Using the rule "half your finished length in beads per warp," I started my necklace by stringing 3" of seed beads on each warp.

TECHNIQUE: DISTRIBUTING FOUR COLORS

Stuck in the Middle

For this necklace, I wanted to combine the cream, black, and bronze of the focal bead with a touch of green. When combining equal portions of four different colors, I like to use two warps of each color with same-color warps placed diagonally across from each other. This setup evenly distributes the colors.

Finished length: 17" (including clasp)

YOU'LL NEED

- Beaded Kumihimo Toolkit

- 12 yd. size 18 nylon string

- 20 grams 8º Japanese seed beads in 4 colors

- Focal bead with hole that fits 8 strands of nylon string

- 8mm endcap set

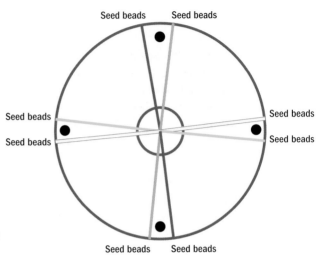

Setup

Cut eight 54" pieces of string, tie them together using an overhand knot, and lock the warps on the disk in the standard starting position. If you're using multiple colors of warp, write down which color you put in each position or take a photo.

On each warp, string 47 8º seed beads (see "Kumihimo Math" to learn how I arrived at this number). Tie a small knot at the end of each warp to keep the beads from falling off and wind each warp onto a weighted bobbin. If the color of your beads doesn't match the color of the string, it's probably a good idea to jot down which color bead goes on which color string. You'll be glad you took notes when we get to the second half of the necklace.

Braiding

Attach the centerweight and braid a ½" nubbin without beads. Begin braiding with beads, starting with a "top-right down" move. Lock each bead in place by tucking it under the first cross-warp it meets. Continue braiding with beads until you have used all of the seed beads. Braid 1" without beads (just shy of the width of the focal bead). Clip the centerweight just below the point of braiding, remove the bobbins, and remove the braid from the disk.

Adding a focal bead

Pull all eight warps through the focal bead. Remove the centerweight and position the focal bead snugly against the beaded braid. With the beaded braid and focal bead below the disk, pull the loose warps up through the center hole. Lock the warps back on the disk in the standard starting position. If using multiple colors, refer to your starting diagram. Make sure that the warps exit the focal bead neatly. Pull the warps so that they are flush against the face of the disk **[A]**.

More stringing and braiding

Referring to the color notes you took earlier, string 47 seed beads on each warp. Tie a knot on the end of each warp and wind onto a bobbin.

Braid 8–12 moves without adding any beads. (Top-right down is the first move; bottom-left up is the second. Don't count turning.) This will reposition the warps and create the over-under point of braiding necessary to lock the beads into place. This also gives you enough space for the first seed beads. Exactly how many braiding moves to make without beads will depend on the shape of your focal bead. Begin braiding with beads. Lock a bead in place with each move. If the first beads refuse to stay in place, try doing a few more moves without beads first.

Continue braiding with beads until you run out of beads.

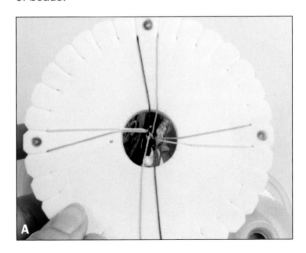

I want my necklace to be 17" long. My pendant is 1" wide and my toggle clasp is about 1" long. Subtracting those from 17", I get 15". That's how long the beaded portion of my necklace needs to be. I divide that by 2 and get 7½" for each side of the necklace. Using the "half your finished length in beads per warp" rule, I need to string 3¾" of seed beads per warp for each half of the necklace. There are usually 12 or 13 8º seed beads per inch, so I multiplied 3.75 by 12.5 and got 47 (rounded up to the nearest whole bead). Voila!

Finishing

Because we counted the beads, the two sides of the necklace should be even, but it doesn't hurt to measure before finishing. When you're satisfied that the necklace is even, braid a ½" nubbin without beads. Remove the braid from the disk and tie an overhand knot. Bind close to the beads. Trim the braid and glue on endcaps as usual.

My pendant is too big to fit into the hole in the disk, and now I can't pull my warps flush. Insert a sharp kitchen knife into the hole of the disk and cut slits in the foam, being very careful not to cut yourself or the braid. I made four evenly spaced ½" cuts. This allowed me to pull the focal bead closer and get my warps flush.

This first bead keeps escaping! Because of the flower shape of my focal bead, one of the first beads added got pushed into the middle of the braid. Easy fix: Just unbraid back to the focal bead. This time when you braid, skip the troubled bead. It's OK. No one will ever know.

TECHNIQUE: MASTERING THE POINT OF BRAIDING

Beaded Pass-Through

This is the most challenging project in this book because you must pay careful attention to getting the warps back in the correct position for braiding after adding the pendant. I say that not to intimidate you, but to congratulate you for coming so far. You're ready. You can do this. I'm assuming that you have read the book and made the projects up until this point. If you're just browsing through the projects, go back to the beginning and start there. No skipping ahead!

Finished length: 18" (including endcaps)

YOU'LL NEED

- Beaded Kumihimo Toolkit

- White glue or fray block

- 12 yd. 1mm satin cord

- 16 grams 6° Japanese seed beads

- Pendant with 6–8mm bail

- 6mm endcap

- Toggle clasp

TIP You'll end up using only about 8 grams of seed beads, but buy extra because the holes of some beads will be too small to fit on the satin cord.

In this project, you'll have two options for adding the pendant: baby steps and giant leap. In the baby-steps option, we'll remove the warps one at a time and pass them through the pendant below the disk. In the giant-leap option, we'll remove all eight warps at once, pass them through the pendant, and then return them to the disk. I think the giant-leap method is easier, but I know it's very scary to take the braid completely off the disk.

Either way, it's critical that the warps be arranged at the correct point of braiding before the braid resumes. The focal bead and accent beads don't touch each other in this design. That leaves exposed braid on either side of the focal bead that will show any inconsistencies.

Setup

I used a spiral pattern in my necklace, so I put color A in the North and South positions and color B in the East and West positions. The North and South warps carried the seed beads. Follow my lead or create your own design, but be sure to write it down or take a photo and note which color warps have beads.

Cut eight 54" warps, knot them together using an overhand knot, and lock them on the disk in the standard starting position. Warps in the North and South positions will carry seed beads. If you're not using the same color pattern as I am, be sure to write down the starting position of each color or take a photo for reference. Wind each warp in the East and West positions onto a bobbin. Stiffen the end of each warp in the North and South positions by dipping it in glue and rolling it to a point. Allow to dry. On each of these warps, string 20 6° seed beads and wind each warp onto a bobbin. Using weights is optional because of the thicker stringing material, but I still like to use them.

Braiding

Braid 4" without beads and then begin braiding with beads. The seed beads aren't that much bigger than the satin cord that carries them, so it can be a bit tricky getting them to stay put. Lock each bead under the first cross-warp it meets. If one pops out, unbraid to it and put it back in place. When you are out of seed beads, braid 1½" without beads. This is where the pendant will sit.

Adding the pendant

Stop braiding after completing a "bottom-left up" move (not the usual stopping point). Scoot the warps back to the standard starting position. If you're using a different color pattern than I am, refer back to your notes and, if necessary, braid a few more moves to get to where you need to be.

Baby-steps option

Position the pendant below the hole in the disk. Start with the left-side North warp and work clockwise. Remove the first warp from its slot, bring it down through the hole in the disk **[A]**, through the pendant (moving left to right), back up through the hole in the disk, and return it to its slot **[B]**. Repeat for each warp. Yes, things will get a little messy **[C]**.

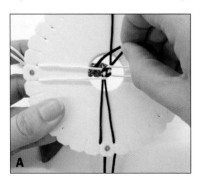

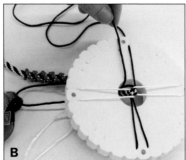

I did it one warp at a time, very carefully, but still everything looks messed up! What happened? Even though we're taking our time and trying to keep everything in its correct place, warps get crossed inside the pendant. It just happens. In projects like Five Marbles and Stuck in the Middle, we could ignore this because the seed beads sit tightly next to the focal bead, but this time we must fix it. Here's how I did it:

One warp should never wrap around another, but the black warp is wrapped around both South white warps. I corrected this by removing the black (lower East) warp from its slot and pulling it up from under the two white South warps. Then I put it back in its slot. On to the next problem.

I have a black (upper East) warp that is over where it should be under. Easy fix: Just pull the white warp (right-side North) out of its slot, pull it so it's no longer tucked under the upper-East black warp, and return it to its slot. If everything looks good, unbraid a few moves to check your work.

The black (upper East) warp is over where it should be under.

The lower East warp is wrapped around both South warps.

It's unlikely that your tangle will look exactly like mine. Refer to the detailed point-of-braiding explanation on p. 82 to help check that every warp is in the correct position.

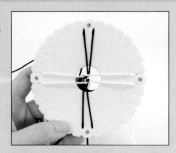

Everything looks good.

Giant-leap option

Clip the centerweight just below the point of braiding, remove the bobbins, and remove the braid from the disk. Pull all eight warps through the pendant. Reposition the centerweight so it is between the pendant and the loose warps, just at the point of braiding.

With the braid, pendant, and centerweight below the disk, pull the loose warps up through the center hole. Referring to your starting diagram, lock the warps back on the disk in the standard starting position.

Check the point of braiding

Pull the warps flush. If the warps are pulled tightly across the face of the disk, it's much easier to see whether yours matches mine **[D]**. Adjust the warps as necessary to re-

create the over-under orientation that creates the braid. Unbraid a few moves to double check that everything is in working order.

More stringing and braiding

On each warp in the North and South positions, string 20 seed beads and wind each warp onto a bobbin. Measure the unbeaded section. Make sure it's 1½" and then braid with beads until you run out. Braid 6" without beads (or until you run out of fiber).

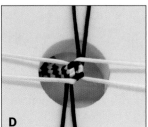

D

Correct point of braiding

Finishing

Measure 6" from the end of each accent bead section and bind the braid. Cut off the excess braid (there's probably enough left over for a bracelet) and glue on endcaps.

Resources

Check your local bead store first. You'll most likely find a large selection of seed beads and interesting pendants and focal beads. If they don't carry kumihimo supplies, be sure to let them know you're interested. Maybe they'll order some for you.

Bead shows are another great place to source materials. I'm lucky to have the Tucson gem shows in my backyard, but even small shows offer artisan glass and beautiful braiding fibers.

Venturing online, your best bets for braiding fibers and endcaps are kumihimostore.com or kumihimotogo.com.

Acknowledgments

To my students, thank you for your support, your questions, and your inspiration! This book wouldn't have been possible without you. Every time I teach, I learn something new.

I also want to thank everyone on the Kalmbach Books team, especially my editor, Mary Wohlgemuth.

About the author

Rebecca Ann Combs has always had a passion for creating and teaching. She is the owner of Design & Adorn Beading Studio in Tucson, Arizona, and has been teaching a variety of classes in jewelry making there since 2008. Her specialty is kumihimo jewelry. She leads a variety of workshops with an emphasis on incorporating beads into kumihimo braids at other venues as well, including the annual Bead&Button Show in Milwaukee, Wis.

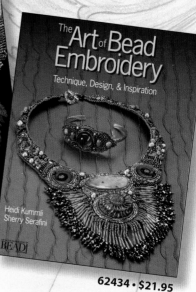
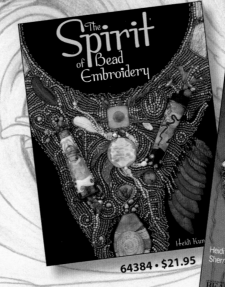